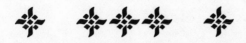

The Purposes
of Groups
and Organizations

Alvin Zander

The Purposes
of Groups
and Organizations

Jossey-Bass Publishers

San Francisco • London • 1985

THE PURPOSES OF GROUPS AND ORGANIZATIONS
by Alvin Zander

Copyright © 1985 by: Jossey-Bass Inc., Publishers
433 California Street
San Francisco, California 94104
&
Jossey-Bass Limited
28 Banner Street
London EC1Y 8QE

Library of Congress Cataloging-in-Publication Data

Zander, Alvin Frederick (date)
The purposes of groups and organizations.

(The Jossey-Bass management series) (The Jossey-Bass social and behavioral science series)
Bibliography: p. 173
Includes index.
1. Social groups. 2. Coalition (Social sciences) 3. Organization. I. Title.
II. Series. III. Series: Jossey-Bass social and behavioral science series.
HM131.Z363   1985   302.3   85-45068
ISBN 0-87589-651-0 (alk. paper)

Manufactured in the United States of America

The paper in this book meets the guidelines for permanence and durability of the Committee on Production Guidelines for Book Longevity of the Council on Library Resources.

JACKET DESIGN BY WILLI BAUM

FIRST EDITION

Code 8545

A joint publication in
The Jossey-Bass Management Series
and
The Jossey-Bass
Social and Behavioral Science Series

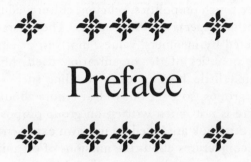

Preface

A group cannot be without a reason for being. This simple fact colors a group's nature because purpose determines how group members function as a body and persist as an ensemble. Due to the ubiquitous connection between a group's characteristics and its purpose, students of social behavior face two questions that have received less thought than they deserve. Why do people create a group? Why do they choose a particular purpose for that entity? Without an understanding of the origins of groups and their goals, we are ill-equipped to explain how members become involved, make plans, and take actions in a body they join.

I became interested in the purposes of groups while conducting a program of investigations into the origins and consequences of group goals on tasks that required physical activity and overt cooperation among members. In those studies, our focus was limited (in order to keep the studies comparable) to quantifiable goals ranging from easy to hard. We examined how members' motives modify the goals they prefer and how group objectives affect members' performances on behalf of their unit.

The ends that members work toward in many organizations, however, are more loosely defined, broader in scope, and more humane than the goals relating to motor tasks that we

asked subjects to work on while studying their goal-oriented behavior. Such general purposes are valuable to society as a whole
because they touch on politics, religion, culture, education, welfare, and other aspects of civilizations. These larger purposes
can be affected by members' values, motives, or emotions, and
by abstract qualities of the organization itself. My earlier research offered little help in understanding such value-related
purposes in groups, so I set out to learn more about them here.
Because there is not much written on group purposes, many of
the ideas in this book are based on my own experience in groups
and on my conjectures about the missions of organizations, not
on the results of scientific investigation. I hope this volume will
stimulate more study of such matters.

A few words about the concepts discussed and the approach used in this volume are in order. A *group* is a collection
of individuals who interact with and depend on one another.
My focus is on an enduring body with continuing characteristics, such as requirements for membership, a name, a charter,
and officers, rather than a temporary association of people
without these qualities, such as a working party, task force,
picnic, crowd, or discussion meeting. Apart from collectives of
brief duration, my interest extends to any kind of organization
that people devise anywhere at any time: for work, play, nurturance, aggression, protection, or whatever. I pay little attention to the size of the body under discussion. Although my
thinking dwells more readily on face-to-face groups, and a majority of the examples in this text describe a group with fewer
than twenty-five members, the fundamental ideas apply to
either a large organization or a small one. I consider effects of
group size in Chapter Five.

A *purpose* of a group is that desirable state of affairs that
members intend to bring about through joint efforts. It is desirable because members foresee the satisfaction they can derive
from moving toward that end and from achieving it. A group's
purpose is based on an expectation about what may happen for
participants in coming days. It is a plan members usually put in
place prior to taking steps for their group's or their own good.
In order to establish a purpose, members must desire certain

outcomes for their unit as a whole or for participants as individuals and must be reasonably confident they can help the membership attain those ends. The impact of a group's purpose on its members depends, at the very least, on whether they know about it. If the objective is known by many participants alike (which at once grants it a degree of validity) and if it describes a course that is understood and commonly accepted by members, the shared view has the weight of a vow about how they intend to behave in that organization. Ideally, a member expects everyone to adhere to the requirements this implied pledge places on all.

In parts of this book I comment on the characteristics of a unit's purpose, such as how well attainment of it can be measured, how difficult the objective is, or how flexible it is. Most readers tend to think of a clear (measurable and acceptable) objective as a *goal*, and an unclear (immeasurable and inaccessible) aim as a *purpose*. I follow that usage here, using the term *goal* when the objective is precise and *purpose* when it is not. The terms *objective, aim, target* are used interchangeably when the above distinction is not relevant.

The objective of this volume is to examine the purposes of groups and to explain, in an orderly fashion, where these purposes originate and what effects they have. The book will encourage readers to pay more attention to the objectives of individuals who engage in group action. Students of group life will find concepts, assumptions, and testable hypotheses here that they can employ in studying the aims of people in organizations. Practical-minded persons will find information they can use when organizing a social entity, establishing its rationale, or selecting activities for it. The audience for this volume includes scholars, organizers, managers, consultants, trainers, and other group facilitators.

Plan of This Book

Chapter One provides a summary of the main ideas in this monograph, drawn together under a series of generalizations—an overview of the book's content. Chapter Two explores the varied purposes of groups in both ancient times and today, the reasons for these objectives, and the causes for changes in them. Chapter Three looks at specific trigger conditions that encourage organizers to develop a unit that will be useful to themselves or others. These trigger states include an unsatisfactory situation or an opportunity for rewarding action, an idea of what improvements can be generated through group effort, confidence among members that they can reach these better outcomes, and support that is available to the group from its environment. A group makes events possible that otherwise would not arise. When these occurrences are a potential source of satisfaction to members, they provide incentives for action (joint action in this case) and become purposes of the body.

The characteristics of a given group's purpose and the effects of these properties are the subjects of Chapter Four. A precise objective stimulates better performance than does a nebulous aim or mere encouragement to excel. A goal at the end of a well-defined path generates more involvement of members and elicits better responses from the group than does an objective without ready access. Challenging goals, but not ones that are too difficult, stimulate more productivity than easy targets. An objective with greater power has a stronger influence on members' thoughts and actions. Think of the true believers, workaholics, strivers, and good group members who forgo their personal desires in favor of ones shared with close colleagues. Acceptance of a group's purpose can change members' lives.

Achievement of more important objectives has a wider array of consequences than the attainment of less important ones. And goals that fit together well, or ones that provide equal shares of the group's output for participants, encourage harmony among group members. The content of a specific group's purpose helps people decide whether they wish to join, what the nature and quality of their personal activities will be, what kinds of rules or standards members should develop, which duties should be assigned to which parts of the organization, whether members are satisfied or dissatisfied, or how they evaluate programs in the unit.

Chapter Five examines the methods by which a group's

purpose is selected. This purpose often has an impact on a group's way of life before the group is even formed because those who develop the entity have in their minds an intention for creating it. Their scheme dominates the organizers' plans for assembling joiners and for starting a going concern. In some groups, members take action before they define an objective. They do things that they think will foster teamwork and are easy to perform, even though the members are not sure where these moves will lead. After completing these actions, they justify their efforts (if necessary) by naming a purpose for them. No doubt such unpurposed efforts occur in organizations, but how often these preclude activities directed toward an earlier established objective is not known. Eventually, if not at the group's outset, members want their unit to have an acceptable objective for its activities, preferably a clear and attainable one. The choice of a group's purpose is the result of a problem-solving process among members and the effectiveness of this selection procedure affects the quality of the unit's aims.

Chapter Six considers how members' values guide their choice of purposes for their group, while Chapter Seven shows how members' motives influence the content of a group's purposes, regardless of whether the motives are for satisfaction with personal outcomes or for satisfaction with the group as a whole, and regardless of whether the group is supposed to do work or is to foster a desired climate or state of affairs for members. People often join a group not only to achieve ends they prize for themselves but also to help the organization as a unit. When members strive to attain something for the group, certain conditions become interesting matters for study. As an example, whether members voluntarily enter and remain in a group or instead are told (by someone with authority) to take up duties there affects the appropriateness and strength of their commitment to the group. A group's objective may differ, moreover, according to whether the members choose it or whether it is assigned by a superior. A group that helps each member meet his own needs (to get well, learn, compose, create) is likely to be different from a unit that asks members to ignore their preferences in favor of the group's demands (to win, produce, earn a profit, recruit new members) or attempts to generate like motives among unlike members.

Chapter Eight discusses conditions that cause members to revise their group's objectives. Individuals move easily from one self-oriented purpose to another and as readily change their behavior. But a group's aim is less often shifted because it is not so simple to change the views of members on a matter that is basic to the existence of the unit and to the core agreements among members and because persons in the group feel an obligation to one another concerning the agreed-on purpose. Members' attempts to fulfill the group's purpose will not diminish until most persons, or at least those in positions of power, agree on a new course and program for the group.

Chapter Nine discusses the activities of groups and how these can be either appropriate or inappropriate to the objectives of that body. Chapter Ten offers advice on how organizers, consultants, and scholars can use the ideas in this essay in their work with groups.

Readers of *The Purposes of Groups and Organizations* will find concepts here that are seldom treated elsewhere, and they will explore ideas that can be helpful in explaining the sources of group behavior. As they review the problems met by leaders, consultants, and scholars who are working to strengthen the aims and efforts of group members, they may be stimulated to explore further the nature of a group's purposes.

Walnut Creek, California   Alvin Zander
August 1985

Contents

The Author

Alvin Zander has been a student of group behavior for many years. From 1948 to 1980 he was a program director in the Research Center for Group Dynamics at the University of Michigan. For twenty of those years he served as director of that center. As professor of psychology and of educational psychology, he has taught courses in the social psychology of groups. During his last seven years at Michigan, he served as the associate vice-president for research. Zander is now retired from academic duties.

Zander earned his bachelor's degree in general science (1936), his master's degree in public health (1937), and his doctor's degree in psychology (1942)—all at the University of Michigan. He developed an interest in group behavior while employed as a graduate student during the Great Depression, helping small towns develop social services that they could not afford to hire from professionals. After a postdoctoral year with Kurt Lewin at the University of Iowa (1942) and nearly three years as a clinical psychologist and a commissioned officer in the U.S. Public Health Service during World War II, Zander returned to the University of Michigan.

Zander has done research on the relations among persons who differ in their ability to influence others, the impact of group membership on a person's self-regard, the nature of identification between persons, the sources of members' motivation to help their group succeed, and the origins of a group's goals. He is coauthor of *Group Dynamics Research and Theory* (1968), has published the results of a program of investigations in *Motives and Goals in Groups* (1971), and has written *Groups at Work* (1977), a discussion of needed research in group dynamics, and *Making Groups Effective* (1982), a guide to fostering the development of well-functioning groups.

The Purposes
of Groups
and Organizations

ONE

Fundamentals
of Group Purposes

Although this book touches on many different aspects of group purposes, the discussion of these separate topics can be subsumed under one or another of several generalizations that summarize the major ideas in these pages. At the outset, let us consider each of these generalizations in turn and thereby provide ourselves with a brief preview of the volume's contents, descriptions of its basic concepts, and a framework for examining the relations among these notions. This overview of the book's highlights also reveals the pattern among the major conclusions drawn from these chapters. The content of these generalizations might suggest to students of groups what the central assumptions of a formal theory concerning the purposes of groups could be.

A group is organized, putting it simply, because it is useful for the organizer, for those who become members, or for bystanders. As a result of their experience with that body, individuals who have a stake in the group become concerned about its fate. This brings us to our first concept about the purposes of groups.

Individuals form a group if they believe a specific situation should be changed and that one person acting alone cannot create that change.

1

The condition they wish to modify may be an unpleasantness, on the one hand, or an awareness that currently adequate conditions might be improved, on the other. It may be a defensive response to a repulsive circumstance or a recognition that conditions provide an opportunity either to accomplish a valued end or to help others do so. An observer who has become aware of the need for change is likely to organize a group if several additional things can be perceived. Creation of a group is preceded by at least four facilitating circumstances:

1. *Conditions in the environment or in the behavior of influential persons are unsatisfactory or offer an opportunity for favorable change.* Circumstances that cause people to form groups include hostile attacks, emergencies due to acts of nature, opportunity for seizing valuable property or for catching animals, dependence on gods, injustices caused by other groups, membership in a class that has little influence, loss of goods to other persons, belief that certain values need wider enforcement, need for regulation, desire for mediation between rival groups, chance for personal financial gain, or wish for improvement in personal skills or health. Through the creation of groups, people develop new ways of making affairs satisfactory for themselves, as time goes by, and better means for relieving difficulties; but no one yet knows all of the kinds of situations that lead to the formation of these entities.

2. *A satisfactory state of affairs is conceived by organizers.* Those who create a group believe not only that something is amiss but also that something can be done to improve matters. They may develop this plan prior to writing a group's charter and recruiting members, or they may postpone detailed planning until they have called together potential members who will help prepare the group for its life-to-be. In either event, they want a satisfactory schema for a group before they attempt to organize.

3. *Organizers and members believe their joint actions will succeed if they try to achieve the proposed better state of affairs.* Although some activities cannot be performed well by a group (writing a report, solving a complex problem, making a sale), others are best completed through such joint effort (solv-

ing a problem that requires creativity, building a structure, collecting money for charity, running a ship, coaching a team). An organizer must be confident and able to persuade others to accept that the desired state of affairs can be achieved through the work of this group. Participants develop faith in their unit by having a say in planning its direction and activities.

4. *Conditions in their community encourage persons to establish a unit and to take part in its activities.* Given the presence of the preceding three conditions, a group is most likely to be developed if people in the community are willing to join groups, tolerate ambiguity during the early days of a group's life, favor values in the community that support a particular group, forgo interest in keeping things just as they are, and develop the knowledge and skill needed for being a member. Moreover, interest in creating and joining a group tends to be greatest if the environs are stimulating, that is, if people live in a complex society where groups are common and valued.

In contrast, persons who are aware of a need for change will not create a group if they cannot conceive of a better state of affairs, do not think a group can attain such a state, are not willing to join any group, have no skill in being a group member, have values opposed to those of potential members, or have no tradition that fosters formation of groups.

An organizer of a group may believe that each of these four conditions is present and may have enough social power to define the undesirable state of affairs, plan a solution, assign specified individuals to membership, give them roles in the group, and prepare the purposes and procedures for that unit.

Developers of a group must declare a purpose for the body they organize.

Individuals who create a group because they believe it will generate a better state of affairs have at the same moment invented an initial purpose for that organization. A group cannot begin or survive without a purpose—a reason for its existence. This purpose is significant to members because it describes what will happen if they do certain things. Their expectations may be the result of a joint agreement or of a proposal made by a superior. In either case, it needs to engender acceptance among members. The stronger this support, the more the purpose has weight and the more pressures members place on one another to do what is necessary toward that end. If participants approve of the objective, they tend to believe they can create the outcome they desire. A group may have several purposes, and participants may move their attention from one to the other of these. A given purpose may lose favor or never be supported by members, but most objectives are accepted and have an impact on their behavior.

If a group's purpose lays few practical requirements on participants because they do not understand it, do not accept it, or have not had it explained to them, individuals will be more interested in personal benefits from membership than in the fate of the group. Their concern with private gains may have either favorable or unfavorable consequences for them as individuals. The effects will be positive if the group was originally created to facilitate individual growth, as in a study-group, self-help counseling agency, or multi-arts studio. The effects will be negative if each person interferes with others' self-oriented moves.

Responsible members who conceive, define, and describe the purposes of a group may attach particular properties to these objectives. Here are some of these characteristics.

- *Measurability:* The degree to which members can reliably determine the group's attainment of its objective
- *Accessibility:* The degree of confidence among members that their chosen joint activities will lead the group toward its objective
- *Importance:* The amount of impact on conditions inside or outside the group caused by members' efforts to reach the group's goal
- *Power:* The extent that the group's purpose is a source of influence on the behavior of members
- *Flexibility:* The ease with which the goal can be changed.
- *Consonance:* The degree of fit among several group purposes
- *Difficulty:* The amount of energy, ability, time, or resources required to achieve a given purpose
- *Cooperativeness:* The amount that each member's gain is

contingent on the output of the group but independent of each person's personal score

Members may prefer particular properties of purposes. They probably favor an objective that is measurable rather than unmeasurable, accessible rather than inaccessible, powerful rather than weak, flexible rather than rigid, difficult rather than easy, cooperative rather than competitive, or important rather than unimportant. However, participants in a group devoted to furthering abstract ideas may want an unmeasurable and inaccessible goal rather than the opposite. Those in a group dominated by dogma will prefer an inflexible purpose. And those with a strong desire for group success will want a challenging goal rather than one that is too hard or too easy.

Different characteristics of group purposes cause contrasting events in groups. An unmeasurable or inaccessible goal generates more confusion and inefficiency than a measurable or accessible one. A powerful goal, or an inflexible one, allows less variation in behavior among members (and thus less creativeness, perhaps) than a rigid objective. A challenging goal causes more effective behavior than a simple or difficult one. A cooperative goal generates more group-oriented behavior than a competitive one. And consonant purposes stimulate more cooperative action than those that are dissonant. Such conjectures, and the conditions that modify them, warrant more study than they have received.

An individual is more likely to join and remain a member of a group that has a purpose.

If persons are to become members of a group, they must know its purpose. If they are required to join an organization, they will want to know the goal of the assigned group and will not participate in it wholeheartedly until they understand these aims. When potential recruits do not know why a group exists, they are less attracted to membership in that entity because they foresee confusion there. They will not be sure, for instance, why they are to perform tasks assigned to them, whether they can satisfy their personal aspirations, how they can evaluate the performance of the group as a whole, or what others are to do in their roles.

A group without a purpose cannot provide satisfaction for members, and people do not often commit themselves to a situation where means to satisfaction are not available. It follows, then, that an individual who has strong self-oriented motives will more strictly require that a group have a relevant purpose before joining it. A group will be less able to recruit members if its purposes have little meaning for the needs of potential belongers.

Members are more willing to remain as members if the group's purpose provides an incentive for them.

Belonging to a group is attractive to members if the purposes of that body promise future satisfaction. This satisfaction may result from achieving personal wishes or from fulfilling desires for the good of the group as a whole. Members leave a group if it offers little fulfillment of such incentives. And if they are forced to remain in the body even though they would prefer to leave it, their participation will be uninspired. If a group's purpose provides no true incentive for members, they are likely to seek ways to make it satisfying. An incentive will be stronger, we presume, if members participate in choosing it and come to a decision that the majority of the group supports.

When participants differ in the purpose each wants the group to have, they try to reduce these differences and to develop a common point of view.

If a group's purpose is to be useful to them, members must know its aim and agree in their interpretation of it because they will move in dissimilar directions, even conflicting ones, if their ideas differ about the group's objective. A unit's purpose is more likely to be useful for all if deciders agree what the aim should be for a body as a whole than if they choose goals that will satisfy only the self-oriented wishes of members. Furthermore, a shared decision about a common objective for the unit is seen by those who take part in the planning to be correct, proper, and attractive because it is a product of their joint deliberation and is a person-to-person pledge for that body. The fact that members have accepted one another's beliefs toward a common end causes each participant to accept the shared ideas of colleagues as a prime basis of truth. As a result of such events, a group's purpose tends to be approved by members, and each expects associates to act in accord with that purpose. Because all feel it is proper to accept the group's purpose, they give that objective common support.

The strength of this support is more potent as the cohesiveness of the group is greater. Its cohesiveness is indicated by the strength of the members' desire to remain as members. The pressure among members to adhere to the group's purpose is greater if the group benefits outsiders than if it serves the separate needs of separate members. Also, interpersonal forces to foster the group's purpose are weaker if members are assigned to a group that has a goal established for it by an authority. In such a case, participants pay more attention to what that powerful individual wants than to what the others prefer. An entrepreneur who creates a group to meet personal needs (for example, starts a new business firm) must convince recruits, perhaps through bargaining over wages and duties, to give up their individual aims in favor of those required by the group. Members' views become similar if this bargaining is successful.

The quality of the problem-solving procedures used by those who organize or join a group may modify the content of the purposes defined for that body.

If members use ineffective procedures when drafting a charter for their organization, the group's purpose may be poorly defined, ambiguously described, or based on assumptions unsuitable for that group. Appropriate decision-making methods can improve the ways that imagination and intuition are brought to bear on selecting a goal. Appropriate ways also help responsible members explicate the group's identity, choose the best means for maintaining harmony among members, and make sure that all have access to the floor.

Decision makers' values limit their freedom of choice when they select a purpose for their group.

Values are concepts about an ideal kind of behavior. A member's values help that member assess the goodness or badness, rightness or wrongness of actions by colleagues, by self alone, or by the group as a whole. Values forbid disapproved behaviors or beliefs more often than they encourage approved ones. Organizations that differ in the values held by members also differ in their aims and actions. The values of a society change from time to time, whereupon a group's purpose changes accordingly.

The motives of those who create or join a group influence the purposes they choose for that organization.

A motive is a person's capacity to find satisfaction in a given state of affairs and a disposition to seek that satisfaction. When a motive is aroused, it stimulates action of an individual in accord with this disposition. A member may have a motive for personal gain or for the benefit of the organization as a whole—a self-oriented motive or a group-oriented desire. The stronger the motive (or desire), the more a member behaves in conformity with it. Its strength is increased if a given state of affairs is seen as more likely to satisfy that motive and if this state can more probably be reached through particular actions. Examples of personal motives are needs for achievement, social power, help, knowledge, security, self-esteem, affection, beauty, approval, artistic output, and recognition. Members' desires for their group concern achievement, fun, nurturing, acceptance, interdependence, mutual assistance, protection, creative interaction, or counseling.

A person who possesses a particular personal motive defines an end state that will, if attained, provide satisfaction. This state is called an incentive, purpose, or goal. It may be a score in a game, financial gain, number of products made, count of souls saved, total concerts presented, or firmness of self-esteem. Members who have a given desire for their group want that unit to generate a condition that will be a fulfillment of that desire or at least not a contradiction of it. They may wish the group to score a number of points, win all its contests, add a quota of new members, care for sick persons, create a sense of fun, distribute food baskets to the poor, or defeat an enemy. These aims are (or allow definition of) group incentives, purposes, or goals. In short, the motives of members help them designate what goals they will favor for themselves or their group. Generally speaking, persons choose an objective that is most likely to provide satisfaction if attained and least likely to cause dissatisfaction if failed.

A group's charter may contain purposes that do not influence the behavior or beliefs of members.

A group can have a stated purpose that is ignored within that body. Members may not understand it, learn to have no need for it, believe it has served its function and thus can be set aside, or prefer other goals instead of it. We assume that members have not accepted a purpose of the group if their beliefs or behaviors are not in accord with that aim. This assumption may not be operational if the purpose is ambiguous, large in size, or takes much time to attain. Members also have rejected a purpose if their behavior or beliefs oppose movement of other members toward that end. Thus an empty purpose may remain in a group's by-laws and be cited as one of its prime objectives.

Members do not change a group's purpose if they believe they will derive adequate satisfaction from actions to fulfull it.

Members initially select a group purpose if they believe they will be pleased by attaining that end. They hold to that purpose as long as their faith in eventual satisfaction persists, and they drop it if they lose confidence in their ability to reach the end they seek for that group or if they realize that the goal is not as satisfying as they had assumed it would be.

Members evaluate the quality of their group's performance by comparing its output to the state of affairs being sought. If the discrepancy is great, they change the group's ways of work or purpose, whichever is easier and promises more satisfaction. It is less difficult to change a group's purpose, we might guess, if that objective is more measurable and accessible. Any of a number of conditions may cause members to lose their enthusiasm for the group's original aim: events that led to the group's formation are no longer important, members' needs are sated, they believe the group is failing and will do so again, or different aims have become more salient to them. Responsible members who consider modifying the group's mission may be prevented from doing so because influential persons in the environment oppose it, members are against it, actions of the group are successful, purposes are too nebulous to modify, a change will cause too much conflict among members, or values in that community oppose change.

Members are more attracted to a difficult goal than to an easy one.

When members choose a goal for their group out of a number of potential ones arrayed along a scale of difficulty, from easy to hard, they tend to prefer harder goals rather than easier ones. They have this preference because they anticipate more satisfaction from achieving a difficult target than from reaching an easy one. They also believe they will be more embarrassed by failing an easy goal than by failing a difficult one. All in all, stronger forces press members toward choosing harder aims.

As a result of these considerations, members prefer for their group a goal that will provide as much satisfaction after a success or as little dissatisfaction after a failure as is possible. They tend to raise the difficulty of their group's goal after a success and lower it after a failure. But they raise it more often after a success than they lower it after a failure. Much of the time, consequently, a group's goals are too difficult, and groups fail more often than they succeed.

Members are more attracted to a clear (measurable and accessible) objective than to an unclear (immeasurable and inaccessible) one.

If participants in a group cannot determine whether they have reached the state of affairs they seek because the attainment of this purpose is unmeasurable, and if they do not know how to attain this end because it is not accessible, they foresee that the probability of accomplishing the group's purpose is small. When the group's aim is unclear, they also sense that the likelihood of obtaining satisfaction from membership is small.

In the light of these ideas, we anticipate that members will move toward the establishment of measurable and accessible ends if current ones are ambiguous. Typically, members leave nebulous purposes in place, making no overt effort to erase them, and then devote their attention to aims they have defined more sharply. Thereafter, the more obscure goals, contained in the statement of the group's charter, have little influence on members' actions. A group's more precise aims, however, elicit interest from members. Participants work to fulfill these, and they evaluate the group's performance on how close it comes to reaching them. Members' interest in a clear objective will be stronger as their motive is stronger—they place priority on better means to attain satisfaction and work harder to reach focused goals than to reach vague ones.

Members like appropriate activities more than inappropriate ones.

A group's activities are more appropriate if they lead toward the group's objectives more efficiently and provide more direct, less costly, and briefer ways to achieve the group's goal. Its activities are more likely to be appropriate if the goal is measurable, the goal is accessible, members prefer to be rational, and the group employs sound problem-solving procedures in choosing its activities.

When a group's activities are inappropriate, they are less likely to be satisfying to members. Members will then make efforts, we expect, to take up more appropriate activities. If this shift cannot be managed, they will be less involved and less attracted to the group, and the unit will become less cohesive.

Members' personal motives and goals are influenced by the demands of their group.

What individuals think is important and what they try to accomplish often is a result of what their group expects them to do. It seems reasonable that members will more closely stick to plans made for them by colleagues if they perceive that these actions have instrumental value to the group or if they are strongly pressed by associates to perform in a way they propose. It is evident that members lose much freedom to change their personal aspirations when they are attracted to remain as members. Good group members, in brief, have their goals fixed by their mates and cannot easily modify these when they may want to do so in order to save pride after failing to live up to mates' expectations. As a result, individuals can experience low self-regard generated by requirements of that membership. Cohesive groups can create burdened members.

Summary

The major ideas in this book fall under a number of generalizations. A straightforward listing of these central themes reveals the relationship among them and makes visible the pattern of concepts behind the discussion in following chapters.

- Individuals form a group if they believe a situation should be changed and that one person acting alone cannot create that change.
- Developers of a group must declare a purpose for the body they organize.
- An individual is more likely to join and remain a member of a group that has a purpose.
- When participants differ in the purpose each wants the group to have, they try to reduce these differences and to develop a common point of view.
- The quality of the problem-solving procedures used by those who organize or join a group may modify the content of the purposes defined for that body.
- Decision makers' values limit their freedom of choice when they select a purpose for their group.
- The motives of those who create or join a group influence the purposes they choose for that organization.
- A group's charter may contain purposes that do not influence the behavior or beliefs of members.
- Members do not change a group's purpose if they believe they will derive adequate satisfaction from actions to fulfill it.
- Members are more attracted to a difficult goal than to an easy one.
- Members are more attracted to a clear (measurable and accessible) objective than to an unclear (immeasurable and inaccessible) one.
- Members like appropriate activities more than inappropriate ones.
- Members' personal motives and goals are influenced by the demands of their group.

Additional Readings

Weick, K. *The Social Psychology of Organizing.* Reading, Mass.: Addison-Wesley, 1979. A thorough review of the rational and irrational problems involved in developing a new organization.

Zander, A. *Motives and Goals in Groups.* Orlando, Fla.: Academic Press, 1971. A report on the results of two dozen investigations into the origins and consequences of goals in work groups.

Zander, A. "Team Spirit Versus the Individual Achiever." *Psychology Today,* 1974, *8,* 64–68. Selfless commitment to a team goal operates in the same ways as commitment to personal aims.

Zander, A. "The Origins and Consequences of Group Goals." In L. Festinger (ed.), *Retrospections on Social Psychology.* New York: Oxford University Press, 1980. A summary of the material contained in *Motives and Goals in Groups.*

TWO

Functions
Served by Groups

A group's purpose, we have noted, is a state of affairs that members intend to create through their joint effort. More kinds of objectives exist in more types of groups than we can ever know. Nevertheless, we will benefit from this chapter's discussion, in which we recall several aims of organizations, remind ourselves that members move toward these goals, and remember that purposeful actions largely determine the nature of a group. In Chapter Three, we consider conditions that favor the formation of a group.

Groups in Early Times

We begin with an examination of reasons for groups in early history, concentrating on established units rather than temporary gatherings. We do not accept the view expressed by Hobbes that human beings were savages before social organizations modified their conduct through force, morality, and law, or that humans accepted social pressures only because they were frightened into obeying the wishes of superiors whose might was right. We believe that people often formed groups because it was useful somehow for them to do so. Spinoza describes the prime value of a group as follows: "Since fear of solitude exists in all men—because no one in solitude is strong enough to protect himself and procure the necessaries of life—it follows that men by nature tend towards social organization" (Durant and Durant, 1963, p. 651). If people created groups when they had a reason for doing so, what were social bodies designed to accomplish in ancient times?

Consider the kinds of groups developed during the period from 300 B.C. to 1500 A.D. Boorstin (1983), Durant (1935, 1939, 1944, 1950), Funk (1982), George (1968), and Stone (1975) comment on the units people organized during those years. Each entity was probably a new kind of group at the moment. In the oldest societies about which we have reliable information (Arabic, Chinese, Egyptian, Greek, Indian), families banded together to create tribes if the male or female parent was a descendant of a common ancestor or if they worshipped the same deity, followed a given chieftain, or needed one another for help, protection, or procreation. People in these tribes jointly built walls, dug ditches, ambushed large animals, dragged fish nets, cut timber, stole from neighbors, worshipped gods, or erected shared shelters. The social units also provided means for effective collaboration when dealing with dangerous situations, such as fires, enemies, beasts, and natural disasters. Tribes joined to form a larger collective called a *clan,* and a wider community then became necessary to control relations between clans. People clung to a family in peace, to a clan in crisis. In special geographical areas where flooding of rivers was common (Egypt and China), large numbers of people were co-opted by powerful strangers to build dams and to distribute the stilled water for irrigation. Members of widely scattered communities were thus brought under the control of one centralized authority that then supervised persons in the larger district. Workers were governed by officials in distant headquarters and ruled by an early form of bureaucracy.

In China, because of such a centralized government, elaborate standards of proper behavior among workers and methods to enforce these standards were developed as early as 300 B.C. "An urban proletariat organized with its masters into industrial guilds. . . . These . . . limited competition and regulated wages, prices, and hours: many of them restricted output in order to maintain prices for products. The guilds undertook functions which . . . citizens of the West have since surrendered to the state: they passed their own laws, and administered them fairly; they made strikes infrequent by arbitrating disputes of employees and employers through arbitration boards representing each side equally; they served in general as a self governing and self disciplining organization for industry" (Durant, 1935, p. 777). Guilds were common for tradesmen, such as barbers, cooks, and coolies, and even for beggars. Members of these unions pressed their brothers to follow strict rules of decorum. Such guilds have survived until today—more than two thousand years.

Athens, about 450 B.C., had the fullest democracy the world has ever known (but available to only a few). Voters did not belong to political parties. Instead, they formed clubs and tried to influence through these the views of legislators concerning religion, military, labor, drama, or politics. The most powerful organizations were created by wealthy men to work against granting the vote to persons in middle and lower classes.

Clubs to counter the opposition of the rich were formed by disenfranchised merchants, workers, and sailors. These latter resented the efforts of the wealthy and their control of the law-making assembly and senate. The action-groups also provided an income for sick members and collectively contracted for labor to be done through teamwork. The clubs conducted a war of ideas against powerful citizens by publishing poems, plays, and pamphlets about the excessive benefits available to those in the upper strata of society. Protesters developed their own version of a legislative body so they could define their complaints more sharply and advocate actions for the government to take on these issues.

In Rome at that time, being a citizen and a member of the army were one and the same. The army made laws for the nation and defended the country. It elected officials to represent specific sets of soldiers. Two officials simultaneously shared a major office for one year. Each officer checked on the other's actions. A *tribune,* a group of ten men, was elected to protect citizens from the government. The ten reported to resi-

dents of the city about events in the senate, vetoed unwise decisions by the senators, made sure that people had fair trials, provided pardons for condemned criminals who deserved them, and
gave asylum to persons needing protection or special care.

By 50 A.D., slaves, who constituted one-fourth of the
population of Rome, sought to relieve their condition through
creating collectives called *collegia*. These were specialized organizations with separate subdivisions for each of many trades
or types of labor. Among musicians, for example, trumpeters,
horn players, tubaists, and flutists had their own distinct locals
—a separate one for each instrument played. Such groups, like
similar ones in Greece, provided mutual help, excursions, and
emergency funds for their members. These unions were trans-
formed into political organizations when demagogues began to
purchase members' votes, a form of bribery that helped destroy
democracy in Rome. Because of their longing for better social
conditions, the worker collectives welcomed Christianity when
that religion reached Italy, and they became the main means
whereby it entered and pervaded Roman society. Christianity
promised a better quality of life in the future—soon for the living, later for the dead. This was a rare emphasis for inventors of
religions at that time but had been a familiar theme in earlier
centuries in other lands.

Christianity popularized worship in groups for the first
time. Saint Paul traveled widely organizing congregations in
Mediterranean countries and continued thereafter to give organizational advice to these churches through his epistles. He urged
church leaders to do things that would keep their groups alive
and counseled inferiors to obey their masters, even if these superiors were cruel or were bad managers. Early Christianity did
not want to antagonize secular authorities.

As the Christian church became a larger and stronger institution with more focused administration of its separate congregations, it began to sponsor many associations that had not
been seen previously. Separate bodies were organized for each
of several objectives—to legitimize certain interpretations of
holy writings, identify and derogate heretical ideas, establish a
consistent content for the Christian creed, punish persons who

disagreed with this creed, build temples large enough for all religious activities of a district, support efforts of a minority to solicit death and martyrdom for themselves, provide sanctuaries for persons who wished to retire from secular life, furnish military protection for Christian crusaders in Palestine, recover land occupied by Moslems, offer martial services in behalf of Christianity and, during the Renaissance, run the state as well as the church, including armies, schools, hospitals, police, and financial agencies.

In order to move trade goods over open terrain, caravans a mile long, with 4,000 camels and hundreds of herders, transported shipments between Southern Arabia and Egypt. The trains inspired an enterprise that fielded gangs of mobile thieves. These crews raided the convoys, pirated their goods, and took merchants as slaves. About 970 A.D., a different kind of unit, called the Sidjistani Society, was formed in Baghdad. The group met for the discussion of philosophical problems, and persons of all nationalities were welcome to take part. The Brethren of Purity was later established to study and compare Greek philosophy, Christian ethics, Sufi thought, mysticism, Shia politics, and Moslem law. Truth, these savants assumed, comes more readily from a meeting of many minds than from the meditations of a single scholar. The group eventually issued fifty-one tracts presenting the world's first unitary system of science, religion, and philosophy.

Beginning in the second century, philanthropic societies were established in Jewish communities of European and Middle Eastern nations, and these in turn founded hospitals, orphanages, poorhouses, and homes for the aged. They provided ransom for prisoners, dowries for financially straitened fathers of would-be brides, and funds for funerals and burials. The synagogue was the community center. It published laws, collected taxes, settled strained interpersonal relations between citizens, provided lodgings for travelers from foreign lands, and sponsored a school where boys studied from dawn to dusk.

In Scandinavia, it was understood that only the bravest military men would enter the hall of the chosen (Valhalla) after death, and a warrior's sins would be forgiven if he died while fighting for his group. Thus, soldiers developed a furious form of battling known as the berserk's way (*berserk gangen*). To be *berserk* was to be dressed in a bear's shirt—that is, to fight without the protection provided by metal armor available as regular issue to men in the armed forces. Scandinavian gangs in small ships specialized in exploring the northern oceans and in robbing homes and churches in many lands, even along distant shores of the Mediterranean and down the Elbe and Danube rivers.

The way of life known as feudalism began in Europe when lords moved their homes to the country to avoid crime in the cities (600 to 1200 A.D.). Serfs in the employ of a baron placed their huts as near his mansion as possible so they might be protected from raiding groups of horsemen scourging the countryside. A parcel of land was rented to each man, and residents created platoons to plough their combined acreage and build dams, dikes, drainage ditches, and roads. Hay in pastures and timber in forests were shared alike by those in the community. Sports teams from one village competed against those from another in contests resembling modern football, hockey, and wrestling. By the year 1000, walls had been built around many of these towns, and assemblies of citizens and officials, called *communes,* were created (over the resistance of the lord) to regulate the affairs of the district and to resist taxes or tolls laid on them by superiors. This was the first democratic governing body since the days of Tiberius in Rome. It fed a new interest in representative government and in individual enterprise.

In the 1200s, traders in countries of northern Europe formed trade associations called *Hanses.* The Hanses of several nations joined forces to protect their shipping against pirates, promote cooperation in commerce between countries, provide a congenial place for sailors and salesmen to stay when away from home, accommodate to the effects of fluctuating currencies, control trade, regulate fishing, adjudicate disputes among members, and finance lawsuits. This Hanseatic League, as it came to be called, also made laws to regulate commerce and enforce honesty in business. These laws were the first attempts legally to control large business firms and, according to Christopher Stone (1975), were no more successful in constraining the actions of large companies than such legislation is today. As is often the case, the league's purposes shifted over the course of several centuries; and it became an oppressive organization, engaging in questionable commercial practices, forcing cities to join the league against their will, creating selfish monopolies, and controlling trade to its own advantage.

In Southern Europe, by the year 1400, guilds of workers had been around for a thousand years; there were guilds of merchants, bankers, physicians, druggists, furriers, tanners, armorers, and members of other fields. These unions were strong enough to outdo the city government in the competition for controlling citizens' behavior. Thus they enforced restraint of trade, tariffs against goods of outsiders, local monopolies, and other self-serving practices. They also paved streets; built docks; fixed harbors; regulated hours, wages, and conditions of labor; set standard prices; inspected the quality of goods; and ran the towns. A guild required its members to follow its rules, not those of the city, and to settle disputes in the guild's courts, not in those of the town. Voluntary groups to help the needy existed in many places outside the world of business. Florence, for example, had seventy-three organizations devoted to works of charity. Many of these are still operating. One set of eleven men ran the clock for the city of Darmstadt. Because few individuals could afford a timepiece or read the time, the hours were indicated, as a public service, by the ringing of bells.

Around the year 1200, student guilds arose in universities to provide protection and power for learners in their relations with professors. These bodies had extraordinary control over the teachers. Members of a student union boycotted bad mentors, paid the salaries of faculty, required professors to swear obedience to the leader of the student union, regulated hours of appearance before classes, fined teachers for not covering material they had agreed to teach, evaluated the skill of each lecturer, and reported deficiencies to members of the student organization.

King John II of Portugal appointed the first advisory

council for evaluating a research proposal (in 1484). This committee was asked to examine a plan prepared by an Italian named Christopher Columbus, to reach Asia (in the east) by sailing westward across the Atlantic Ocean. The council advised the king not to provide the funds sought by Columbus because they believed his estimate of the distance across the Atlantic was too low. A second committee could not decide what to recommend. The queen of Spain settled the matter by making a grant to Columbus on her own.

Printed books, when they first became available, were a noteworthy stimulus to intellectual activity in groups. Because few workers could make out printed words, a number of colleagues would hire a skilled person to read aloud to them while they quietly did their jobs. Men in taverns likewise enjoyed listening to a rendition of a text they had chosen (a forerunner of radio, television, or the jukebox). Radical books and essays on religion, read to groups outside the church, excited discussion among the attendees, and these meetings, Boorstin (1983) thinks, stirred the beginnings of the Protestant Reformation.

What observations shall we make about this odd sample of organizations? We see, first of all, that humans established entities centuries ago for many reasons.

1. In response to fear, anger, and hostility. Families created tribes and clans for greater efficiency in defending themselves. Feudal villages and student guilds provided protection for members as well. Tribes, clans, cities, and nations organized armies to fight one another; and men were assembled everywhere, over and over, for this ever-present kind of unit.

2. To make sure that people were fair to one another. A balanced distribution of such resources as land, wood, water, wages, or workers was agreed on by families, guilds of laborers, courts, or associations of tradesmen. Distribution of labor was equalized by family councils, guilds, or communes of feudal villages. And rules for ensuring fair wages or hours of work were set by the same kinds of units.

3. To provide care for the social welfare of members through

loans, unemployment benefits, life insurance, or bridal funds, as exemplified by guilds in ancient Greece and Rome and by synagogues in European communities. Hospitals, refugees, and schools were developed by comparable organizations.

4. To complete tasks too big or heavy for one person. Companies in construction, farming, shipping, lumbering, or manufacturing came into being for this purpose.

5. To help men clarify their thoughts, initially in Greece but later in Arabia, where the writings of the Greeks were compared with fashionable beliefs of a later day, and again during the Renaissance, when rational thinking and new ideas in art and science led many to turn for the first time from religious dogma as the basis for all wisdom.

6. To worship a deity. The most frequent assemblages (aside from armies) were congregations for this purpose. Large institutions were created to spread and defend doctrinal views.

7. To make laws for the family, tribe, clan, assembly, senate, business league, guild, church, or synagogue. Lawyers were doubtless as common in ancient Rome as they are in the United States today.

8. To change beliefs of the larger society concerning social problems, social power, or civil rights.

9. To arbitrate disputes between individuals or groups and to decide whether a person was guilty of disapproved thoughts or actions.

In many of these bodies, members made decisions by voting, but we do not know how often participants had the right to speak at meetings. Even when a democratic government existed, as in Greece for a while, interaction among members of the senate was exceedingly ill-mannered. Speakers were howled down, punished for proposing a law that proved to be ineffective, or were directly pressured by members. It often happened, therefore, that a senator who wanted his views to be heard would hire a professional person known as an *orator* to talk for him in the senate. That individual was then the target of any derision.

The basis for interpersonal influence among men in Greece was coercion or reward because logical persuasion, expertness, legitimacy, or attractiveness of the speaker were seldom as effective. Consequently, hierarchies were more common than common councils.

Were events in ancient days dominated by soldiers and priests? Or do the interests of historians and available records cause writers to emphasize the matters that make it seem that way? We cannot answer that question, but force and faith still cause strain in interactions between sets of people and are still the most popular means for solving intergroup problems.

Groups change their purposes over time. The Hanseatic League moved from being a cooperative association of companies to being an oppressive cabal. Roman guilds switched from being unions to being political parties and then to being religious bodies. The Catholic church changed from being a supporter of a faith to being a government of secular activities, a police force, a corporation on an international scale, and back again to being a cross-country religious agency. Feudal villages changed from being centers for small farms to being self-governed city-states.

Although the characteristics of purposes in early social entities are not well known, objectives probably varied in how clearly they were stated, the methods members used in reaching them, the amount of demand they made on the behavior of members, the emotional or rational content of the group's goal, the changeableness or fixedness in aims of the organization, and the effort that was needed to achieve a goal. Such properties of purposes exist as well in today's groups.

Groups in Modern Times

Centuries later, similar group objectives abound, and the interests of organizers are much like those of earlier years. To be sure, we currently have better means of communication, transportation, education, construction, destruction, health care, and warfare, but changes in ways of living have inspired few groupings now that would not have been possible or useful then. Let us review some of the purposes of formal bodies in current settings. The list that follows is not a representative sample; it merely illustrates a variety of outcomes in today's groups.

- To protect members from physical harm (community protective association, emergency squad, platoon in army)
- To solve a problem for members or for those who create the unit (committee, commission, task force, research staff)
- To reduce costs for members (buyers' cooperative, trade association)
- To make resources available (bank, rental agency, personnel department)
- To accomplish heavy or arduous tasks (construction crew, assembly line)
- To make routine individual tasks more tolerable (picking apples, sewing quilts)
- To set rules or standards for others to follow (legislative body)
- To change the opinions of persons outside a group (citizens' action association, professional society, political party)
- To worship a deity (religious body)
- To be reverent toward ideas or objects (patriotic society, veterans' group)
- To heal members and nonmembers (psychotherapy group, staff of surgery)
- To teach persons information or skills (school, tutoring agency)
- To improve a system of ideas or a theory (academic department, professional society)
- To make things for consumers (factory, production line)
- To seek and integrate information (blue-ribbon panel, commission)
- To enrich leisure time of members (hobby club, discussion group, adult education class)
- To give advice to those who seek it (consultant firm, support group)
- To decide on the guilt of peers (jury, Star Chamber)

- To engage in performing arts (orchestra, dance company, drama troupe)
- To capture persons who break the law (police, posse)
- To administer an organization (executive committee, trustees, regents)

There is no way to tell how deficient this list is because there are no adequate records of groups and their goals. Thus we might as well examine several other sets of group purposes, apologizing for their disorderly nature, their incompleteness, and their incompatibility one set with another. Parsons (1960) proposes four types of functions groups serve: acquiring sufficient resources for that body to operate (as in a small shop), implementing goals set by the group (as in a department within a larger organization), preserving smooth collaboration among separate parts (as in a police agency), or supporting cultural values (as in a school or museum). Katz and Kahn (1966) name four kinds of organizations: productive or economic (to provide goods), managerial or political (to coordinate resources), maintenance of the organization or society (to train students), and adaptive (to create new knowledge). Perrow (1961), in an analysis of large organizations, assumes that such bodies have one or more of five goals: (1) to fill the needs of society as a whole by producing goods, providing services, maintaining order, or maintaining cultural values; (2) to provide what the customer or consumer of an organization wants in consumer goods, business services, health care, or education; (3) to ensure appropriate functioning of the organization itself, with an emphasis on its growth, stability, profits, control, or development; (4) to describe the goods or services provided by that institution, thereby emphasizing their desirable quality, quantity, variety, style, availability, or uniqueness; and (5) to indicate proper procedures for the group's activities, such as political moves, community services, training of employees, or responses to rules made by governing agencies. Clearly, this set of categories covers the functions of many organizations.

Visitors to the United States from other countries often tell us that there are more organizations here than in their homeland. Tocqueville ([1835] 1956, p. 19) noted this in 1831 when he toured this nation. He said, "Americans of all ages, all conditions, and dispositions, constantly form associations . . . religious, moral, serious, futile, general, or restricted, enormous or diminutive . . . to give entertainments, to found seminaries, to build inns, to construct churches, to diffuse books, to send missionaries to the antipodes." And, in another place, "If a stoppage occurs in a thoroughfare, and the circulation of vehicles is hindered, the neighbors immediately form themselves into a deliberative body; and this extemporaneous assembly gives rise to an executive power, which remedies the inconvenience before anyone has thought of recurring to a pre-existing authority superior to that of persons immediately concerned. If some public pleasure is concerned, an association is formed to give more splendor and regularity to the entertainment. Societies are formed to resist evils which are exclusively of a moral nature, as to diminish the vice of intemperance" (p. 95).

Tocqueville believed that democracy and equality make men independent and willing to stand on their own feet. They form organizations because they realize they can accomplish more by helping one another without turning to established authority for aid.

Ideas about why people create organizations can be distilled from a volume called *The Encyclopedia of Associations* (Ruffner, 1968). This book, which is brought up to date from time to time, contains descriptions of 13,000 bodies, from tiny to massive, from local to international. Each account gives basic facts about an association's size, age, members, staff, subgroups, requirements for membership, program activities, and purpose. I examined such data for a random sample of 290 associations (1972). These operate in various subject-matter areas: health, business, race relations, foreign affairs, athletics, recreation, numerous professions, and many others. What kinds of outcomes do they seek, regardless of their field?

The number of associations wanting particular states of affairs is shown in Table 1. Some organizations work toward more than one of these. The most frequently sought end is to generate better procedures or methods. Instances include improvement of accounting practices in the hotel business, the development of better methods for feeding hogs, sharing experiences in methods of college administration, and improving procedures for rehabilitating injured muscles. Associations also help members analyze methods for doing work and assist them in developing better ways to function in a given profession or occupation.

Another frequent objective is the development of standards to guide behavior, regulate methods of manufacturing, or dictate appropriate properties of finished products. Examples are ethical standards for professional activities, codes for construction of buildings, and uniformities in manufactured items, such as screws, wires, tires, or pliers. Associations seek also to obtain wider usage of certain beliefs or practices, to increase mutual helpfulness among persons, and to develop improved ideas or theories. Other purposes, such as improving the well-being of individuals, creating effective responses to governmental regulations, and maintaining reverence for specific things and events, interest fewer associations. Note that a prime assumption behind these aims and plans is that improvements can be made by and should be sought by members.

Some of these objectives, called *reflexive,* are for the benefit of members of the association or for the group itself. Others, called *transitive,* are directed toward the good of non-members. Out of the 290 associations in my sample, 201 were reflexive and 89 were transitive. Thus these associations work more often in behalf of members than of nonmembers. Is this contrast in their foci typical of other kinds of organizations? Outcomes pursued for members (reflexive) are improvement of procedures, development of standards, creation of better theories, and provision of mutual assistance (see Table 1). Outcomes turned toward outsiders (transitive) are creating wider acceptance of a particular idea or behavior, improving the well-being of individuals, inducing wise reactions to new laws, and preserving reverent attitudes toward certain ideas or events. Programs for the benefit of nonmembers provide social welfare or urge acceptance of particular beliefs. Activities to help members are concerned with the effective functioning of individuals in

Table 1. Outcomes Desired by Associations and the Beneficiaries of These Outcomes: Members or Nonmembers.
(N = 290)

Desired Outcomes	(1) No. of Assns. with this Outcome[a]	(2) % of N	Beneficiaries of Outcomes					
			Members[b]		Nonmembers[c]		Both	
			Assns. with this Outcome	% of Column 1	Assns. with this Outcome	% of Column 1	Assns. with this Outcome	% of Column 1
Improved methods or procedures	166	57	97	58	36	22	33	20
More precisely stated standards for uniform behavior, practices, or things	87	30	44	51	31	36	12	13
Wider public acceptance of views, practices, things	85	29	27	32	49	58	9	10
Increased amount of mutual helping	66	23	29	44	28	42	9	14
Improved theory or system of ideas	55	19	35	64	9	16	11	20
Improved well-being, health, financial security of individuals	45	16	8	18	36	80	1	2

More effective response to social pressure, laws, and changes in laws	42	15	16	38	22	52	4	10
Maintenance of value of past events, persons, or beliefs	38	13	16	38	22	52	—	—
Improvement in quality of processed objects	36	12	14	39	8	22	14	39
More complete and accurate information	35	12	14	40	19	54	2	6
Feedback concerning attainment of aims	18	6	13	72	2	11	3	17
Increased financial and other resources	14	5	6	43	6	43	—	—

[a] Many associations have more than one outcome.

[b] If members are the beneficiaries of the outcome, the outcome is termed *reflexive.*

[c] If nonmembers are the beneficiaries of the outcome, the outcome is termed *transitive.*

their careers or the improved operation of units that belong to that association.

Its field of activity makes particular outcomes more important than others to an association. Improvement of practice, for example, is most often of interest to trade and commercial associations (70 percent of them); standards and rules are important to athletic or sports societies (62 percent) and to organizations interested in good government (44 percent); mutual helping is stressed by associations devoted to public affairs and civil rights (52 percent) and by those active in social welfare (48 percent); improved systems of ideas are mentioned most often by scientific and professional societies (73 percent).

The 290 associations have been in existence for thirty-four years on the average. The older bodies (mean tenure of forty years) are mainly concerned with government, public administration, the military, or sports. The younger (mean tenure of eighteen years) are largely devoted to public affairs and civil rights. Societies with interests in social fairness clearly are a more recent invention than associations with concerns in governmental matters.

Douglas and Wildavsky (1982) assert that entities interested in protecting the environment have recently increased in numbers because of a growing worry over the use and disposal of toxic wastes and insecticides. In the 1960s, a handful of conservationist associations sought to protect land or wildlife and to press for the establishment of governmental agencies that would better manage the nation's natural resources. Few of those associations had ordinary citizens as members. Today, there are seventy-five national associations concerned with conservation, ecology, and reduction of pollution in the environment. Many of these bodies have thousands of voluntary members in hundreds of local chapters or affiliated groups. New preservationist organizations continue to arise. A special feature of more recent societies is their use of small groups throughout the country, each of which is encouraged to take militant action on local misbehavior.

Because descriptions of group purposes are hard to find, I saved printed accounts describing the formation of new organizations as I came across them in casual reading. I assumed these birth announcements would more often discuss purposes than would stories about already established bodies. By the time I stopped collecting clippings, I had usable ones describing the origins of seventy-two groups. The purposes of these bodies are summarized in Table 2.

Table 2. Purposes of Seventy-two New Groups.

Purpose	Number of Groups
To generate changes in customs of society	18
To work as a group on making a physical object or a situation	14
To change the ways of a large organization	13
To change members as persons	11
To change views of decision makers in the community	8
To improve relations between groups	4
To change the nature of the group itself	4

More than half of the neophyte organizations sought to change the beliefs or actions of persons in their communities. Because the accounts were gathered in the late 1960s and the purposes of the new organizations were apparently influenced by feelings of injustice widespread in those days, interest in social change was probably stronger in the bodies at the time than, say, in the 1980s. Fashions in the functions of organizations change over the years.

A different approach to considering varieties of purpose is to examine the number of parts within formal bureaucracies. Ordinarily, huge organizations take care of government, health, education, defense, postal service, or religion. Modern methods of manufacturing also depend on bodies of great size. Examples of large units are listed in Table 3. Numerical values given there indicate the number of all kinds of smaller bodies contained within the larger unit, the total number of persons who belong to each type, and the date when these figures were ascertained. The contents of this table are from a book by David Funk (1982) in which he discusses how public laws affect the cohesion among members of a group.

Table 3. Number of Smaller Bodies and Members Within
Different Kinds of Organizations.

Type of Organization	Number of Smaller Bodies	Total Number of Members
Active business corporations (1963)	1,323,000[a]	—
Local labor unions (1960)	78,000	600,000
AFL-CIO (1980)	—	16,570,000
Marketing cooperatives (1971)	7,500	—
Farmers' cooperatives (1971)	3,678	—
Credit unions (1973)	22,878	27,552,000
Prepayment health centers (1973)	457	12,000,000
Cooperative apartments (1965)	100,000	—
Condominium apartment buildings (1975)	—	2,000,000
Colleges and universities (1974)	2,600	622,000[b]
Churches (1975)	—	127,000,000
Voluntary social services (1971)	6,000,000	111,000,000

[a]There are 3.6 million inactive corporations.

[b]Members of faculties.

We see in Table 3 that there are more voluntary service associations and religious congregations than corporations, more corporations than we might expect, and many local labor unions, even though, as Funk reports, only 20 percent of the people in the working force of the United States are members of unions. Funk notes that 9 percent of the total labor force (of more than eighty million persons) were self-employed in 1972; thus, 91 percent of employed persons worked as members of a group, not as solo functionaries. The table omits data about many kinds of bodies: small shops, governmental offices, elementary and high schools, and community service agencies.

In the years since World War II, self-help groups, inspired by the success of Alcoholics Anonymous, have arisen to help members deal with personal problems. These groups relieve members' worries about "agoraphobia, alcoholism, arthritis, bereavement, drug addiction, epilepsy, gambling, heart disease, manic depression, radical surgery, single parenthood, or weight management" (Borman, 1983, p. 13). Members burdened by a given condition meet regularly and help one another, often with the assistance of a counselor, to understand their own and others' troubles and to plan ways of finding relief. We get an idea of how widespread self-help groups are when we learn from Borman that in the city of Chicago nearly 700 such groups, covering 150 kinds of worriers, are listed in a citywide directory. Alcoholics Anonymous has 48,000 chapters in 105 countries. An organization for parents of missing children has 300 locals in the United States, a body for parents who abuse their children has 1,500 chapters, and there are more than 3,000 religious cults, all organized in the last decade or so.

Summary

When we review the kinds of groups people form, several conclusions become evident. Individuals create a group when they develop a purpose that collaboration can help them meet. Groups are organized for different purposes, but all units are alike in one respect: they are intended to be useful to members, nonmembers, or both. If groups are to serve a specific function, it follows that the purposes of groups shift as the desires of those who have a stake in the group change—different wishes or interests cause new requirements. Also, when people modify their wants because society experiences changes in religion, climate, transportation, therapy, food, business, laws, or courts, the outcomes they seek from groups move about, and the purposes of their groups change accordingly. So groups of several kinds come and go in different cultures, times, and places. Although they may differ in their aims and activities from site to site and from day to day, many groups exist for similar reasons decade after decade.

Because a group has a reason for existing, its purpose can affect the motivation of members, where they direct their effort, and where they find satisfaction. Whether the group's purpose is the result of a joint decision or is part of a contract to conform with the demands of superiors, the purpose is a public promise among people that they will try to reach a given state of affairs through collaborative activity. Such a plan is quite different from the private intention of an individual person. It is powerful. It is useful in an organization. It is mostly ignored in studies of human behavior.

Additional Readings

Kanter, R. *Commitment and Community.* Cambridge, Mass.: Harvard University Press, 1972. How communes of today and yesterday win the loyalty of their members.

Kauffman, H. *Are Government Organizations Immortal?* Washington, D.C.: Brookings Institution, 1976. If a governmental agency dies, its purpose is often passed on to one that remains.

Lanternari, V. *The Religions of the Oppressed.* New York: Knopf, 1963. The origins, currently, of new religions in less industrialized societies.

Olson, M. *The Logic of Collective Action, Public Goods and the Theory of Groups.* Cambridge, Mass.: Harvard University Press, 1971. A theory about the parts groups play in the economy of this nation.

Stinchcombe, A. L. "Social Structure and Organizations." In J. March (ed.), *Handbook of Organizations.* Skokie, Ill.: Rand McNally, 1965. A review of conditions that foster the formation of groups.

THREE

Conditions
Fostering Group
Formation

Our position is that individuals who organize a group are stimulated by circumstances they wish to improve for the benefit of themselves or others. They assemble a social unit if they believe a given state of affairs ought to be given attention by several persons and if they are confident that a group can bring these changes about. At least four conditions (we shall call them *triggers*) ought to exist if organizers are to become interested in developing a new unit. When any of these trigger states are absent, potential developers are less likely to create a group.

1. *Particular conditions are unsatisfactory or suggest an opportunity for desirable change.* An unfavorable situation, we have seen, often encourages organizers to bring people together to make responses to that circumstance. We recall examples of such assemblages. College students feel that teaching on their campus is not relevant and should be modified to deal more closely with political problems of the day; thus they organize in order to pressure the faculty toward changes in the curriculum. Citizens create groups because of their dislike for air pollution, nuclear fallout, unsafe automobiles, dishonest pharmaceutical firms, or research in genetic engineering. A set

of farmers move about the state attending auctions of farmers' possessions that are being sold because the mortgages on their properties have been foreclosed. The buyers keep their bids low and thereby make it possible for the owners to repurchase their things from the bank. Companies develop new departments to deal with changes in methods for treating numerical data, ethics in selling, or recruiting women. Because the Detroit baseball team is having a winning season, its followers form a society that meets weekly for self-congratulatory luncheons.

In less developed nations today, where natives are exploited by powerful outlanders, religious cults arise to provide hope for those who join them (Lanternari, 1963). Each movement usually is founded by a self-acclaimed prophet who claims to have received revelations from a supreme being, spirit, or dead hero. This founder ordinarily predicts an imminent cataclysm that will precede the raising of the dead, after which there will be a reversal of the existing social order (the poor will become rich and the rich will become poor), banishment of foreigners, the end of this planet, the birth of a new one, and plenty of goods for all.

In the descriptions of neophyte groups I clipped from newspapers and magazines late in the 1960s, the situations that caused participants to create these units were often given. These triggering circumstances are shown in Table 4. We see that most

Table 4. Conditions That Stimulated Formation of Groups.

Condition	Number of Groups
A large organization is engaging in undesirable actions	23
Individuals have personal needs for help	16
A larger organization needs help, is ineffective	11
Problems of society need attention, study, change	10
Replacement of a failing group is needed	8
Specific persons are creating undesirable conditions	3

of the groups in this small sample were developed because organizers were displeased with the programs of a local and influential organization, such as a city council, political party, civic society, university administration, or faculty. Some groups came about because persons in the community needed encouragement, counseling, or psychotherapy. Other triggers included: an organization is failing and should be replaced with a stronger one, views in the larger community ought to be reformed, and powerful individuals should be opposed.

A frequent cause for creation of a group, we noted earlier, is perception of physical danger. Fear, more than any other condition, led families in ancient times to create tribes in which they could protect each other. Hunters traveled in platoons to provide mutual cover against hazards of field and forest. Men joined armed groups when told an enemy was near. Neighbors organized to patrol the area and to stop attacks on their persons. Anxiety among modern soldiers causes them to form into supportive groups (Janis, 1963) and to increase their group's cohesiveness (Stein, 1976). An accepted theory among ecologists who study the origin of communities of animals, such as prairie dogs or deer, is that groupings of creatures arise because one species competes with another for scarce resources in food or space. Only when this kind of rivalry occurs do animals develop an analog of a human community organization (Lewin, 1983a, 1983b).

Organizers also create groups to solve problems or decide about new possibilities: a manager appoints a committee because the firm needs to make new products the company might sell, a group of citizens meet because they are unhappy about the kind of buildings allowed in their neighborhood, a researcher seeks funds to finance the staff of an investigation because current medicines are failing to cure patients and should be replaced by better ones, and parents convene because their adolescent children need clear and similar rules all parents can enforce alike.

A group is developed, in some instances, because the task to be done is too big for one worker and can only be completed or can be done more cheaply, quickly, or better if taken up by several colleagues. Teams created for such reasons are assembly lines, construction crews, restaurant staffs, newspaper reporters, battle parties, orchestras, or coaches of football

teams. A group is more willing to tackle an unpleasant assignment, moreover, if several persons approach the task together.
We see examples of such support in meetings of self-help groups
whose members assist one another to reduce their consumption
of alcohol and food or to engage in psychotherapy. Joggers last
longer if they trot as a crowd. Sets of college students encourage one another in preparing for an examination.

The chance to make money by creating a new business
leads to the formation of numerous groups. In some communities, special agencies discover markets for innovative products or
stimulate the creation of companies that take advantage of
these opportunities. Much of Japan's industrial growth has been
fostered by the Ministry of International Trade and Industry
(MITI), which looks worldwide for evidence about things that
might be sold in undeveloped markets. MITI also helps develop
firms that will make or sell these fresh products. The essence of
their marketing is to find a need and fill it.

We are not surprised when a need for a novel service inspires the formation of a new kind of ensemble. But we may
not recognize that a group can also arise out of a coalescence of
individuals who informally engage in a joint activity. While
working as an assemblage of persons who have a common interest, their output wins appreciation of colleagues who are not in
that set. As a result, the collective earns recognition from the
parent organization, formal status, a name, a working place,
tools, a budget, and whatever else it needs to carry on. Kauffman (1976) remarks that this method of group creation is familiar in government bureaucracies. It occurs, for example,
when an organization adopts new devices (such as a computer
or equipment for storage of data) that in turn generate a desire
for new methods and policies to guide their cooperative use.
Groups also grow out of sets that originally came together to
take joint action temporarily and who later realize they are a
whole and ought to have a goal that justifies their unitary existence.

Individuals who are in a large organization and who favor
deviant ideas or plans are delighted when they find one another.
Within a company, such members often form cliques or cabals

that help them cling to and rationalize their unusual beliefs (Burns, 1955). Black scientists, engineers, and health professionals, for instance, have developed their own professional associations. Some of these arose as much as forty years ago "because segregation, separation of races and discrimination against blacks prevented their full participation in the affairs of society—such as being unable to attend scientific meetings at hotels that barred blacks, or being denied membership in local medical associations" (Malcolm, 1984, p. 48). Other minority societies, created more recently, were not the result of schisms in which blacks went off to form their own groups but were created because blacks became aware they had different priorities and professional interests than whites. Today there are more than forty associations exclusively for scientists and professionals from minority groups in this country.

Throughout history, new groups to sponsor unusual approaches to science, art, literature, or religion have been organized during times of war, economic distress, or the weakening of previously precious values. One sees these innovations in legislative bodies, schools, branches of the military, churches, or companies. Changes in ways of life in a society provide fresh reasons for groups not seen theretofore.

2. *A satisfactory and attainable state of affairs is conceived by the organizers.* Recognition that something should be changed is not enough to inspire persons toward organizing a unit. Developers must also have ideas about what could be done and how things could be different and better. The group purposes we noted in previous pages were conceived by developers as a more satisfactory state than had existed. The invention of a new purpose is, clearly, an intellectual procedure subject to the processes of thinking, social problem solving, personal preferences, and group-oriented motives. The effects of these several modifiers on the choice of a group's goal are taken up in Chapters Five, Six, and Seven.

Stinchcombe (1965) proposes that the tendency of people to form in groups is fostered by special views of organizers. He observes that individuals develop groups most readily when they believe that (a) doing things through group effort provides procedures that otherwise would not be available to members, (b) a desirable activity can be performed most efficiently by a group, (c) members will benefit from this activity, (d) the necessary resources in materials, men, and money are at hand, and (e) outside opposition or resistance to the group's activities can probably be overcome. To put it briefly, creation of a group is a more sensible thing to do when its creators believe it can do what they expect of it.

All in all, groups are formed in any of several ways:

• A problem or crisis brings people together to help one another, improve their actions, or protect their property.
• A person with an idea about what could be initiated recruits colleagues, posts a call for a general meeting, or invites participants to join him or her in a group.
• Like-minded persons assemble around an attractive activity or leader and arrange things so they can continue to meet.
• A set of persons are told to become a group by an individual who has the power to make this assignment.
• Several individuals arouse widespread interest in a topic through information put in the public media, demonstrations, or petitions, and the aroused persons create a unit to keep this interest alive.

The process of organizing is discussed further in Chapter Ten.

Surprisingly often, a group's creation is inspired by one person who initially develops key ideas, assembles sympathetic colleagues, garners necessary resources, and gives the set faith in itself as a social entity. Prophets assemble members of a new cult. Superior officers put employees into subgroups. A committed citizen starts an action group, a union, a community council, an association for civil rights, or a cell to protect the local environment. Men who, on their own, have recruited disciples to work with them include Fidel Castro, Julius Caesar, Jesus Christ, Henry Ford, Thomas Edison, Martin Luther King, Nikolai Lenin, Louis XIV of France, and Henry VIII of England.

Adrian Mayer (1966), an anthropologist, observes that

persons may come together only because each of them is dependent alike on the same focal person. He calls these *quasi groups* because the members do not talk with one another but interact exclusively with this central character. Transactions among those who belong to this kind of unit are not necessary for its survival. Such a quasi group arises when individuals who have previous linkages of friendship, economic activity, or kinship develop bonds with a focal person (perhaps a politician in the midst of an election campaign) and these latter bonds define who belongs to the set. Members have no rights or obligations, and the collection soon dissolves if the focal individual becomes no longer available. The purpose of this kind of group is whatever the focal person asks of the members. Individuals near the center of the set, because they have close relations with the focal one, may eventually replace the central person as the core of the group if they begin to interact with one another rather than with the leader alone and thereby become dependent on each other. In this way a quasi group may change into a more regular unit.

As we have noted, administrators in larger organizations create subunits because they have the responsibility to do so. And due to this duty, they later change such bodies when that seems necessary. Sources of influence on a group (other than the boss) are rival bodies, planning agencies, regulations (for those units whose course of action is constrained by legal requirements), values, and the motives of members (see Chapter Six). An organizer's conception of a satisfactory state often is an idealized notion and difficult to attain. For fear that a too demanding objective will cause members to lose interest in it, the organizer plays down this difficulty and describes the future for the new body as rosier than it probably will be in fact. Or else the organizer proposes for members preliminary actions that they believe will succeed.

Recruiting for a group cannot be based on wholly uncertain plans about the proposed body. Members must have a reasonable confidence in the group's likely output before they will allow themselves to be parts of it. Persons who face an unsatisfactory situation and who wish to reduce its more repulsive aspects or replace them with more attractive features may be unable to think of feasible things to do. When they cannot conceive of an improved condition, they likely will feel that a new group is not worthwhile. In desperation, they may assemble a set of persons to help one another endure the unpleasant condition, punish ones who are responsible for the unfavorable situation, or try exploratory actions toward defining a better state of affairs.

3. *Members believe they will achieve a more satisfactory state of affairs through activities of the group.* One who assembles a new group must give recruits confidence that their unit can accomplish its aims. Barnard (1938) remarks that a manager's task is not only to define the group's purpose but also to make sure it is accepted by members. Peters and Waterman (1982) tell how a good supervisor infuses employees' day-by-day behavior with significance through reminding them that their actions help toward attaining the long-run purposes of the group. Cohen and March (1974) contend that academic departments in a university have vague objectives that differ widely. Accordingly, an executive officer of a university must help participants believe in the overarching purposes of the university because these provide harmonious aims for all departments. The official also must sponsor preparations for fulfilling such goals.

In order to increase members' efforts in behalf of their group, responsible persons make sure that participants know what the purpose is and elaborate on this knowledge through speeches, mottoes, memoranda, conferences, discussion groups, demonstrations, or displays. They make sure that movement by the group toward these ends is visible to all. Moreover, they publicly praise personnel who take steps toward attainment of these joint purposes.

The creation of confidence among members depends on more than a purpose and a set of participants. It also requires that a number of decisions be made about how the group will work, find its members, orient these people, arrange them in a stable organization, and tap their enthusiasm. Imagine how differently members may go about creating a structure for their group in separate organizations, such as those described here. Each of these is a group I once watched being formed.

- A set of consultants who separately serve business firms in a big city meet and agree to develop an informal organization through which they can help one another in their work.
- College students decide that the youth-program at a local church is not what they want, and they plan their own independent group.
- Representatives from all clubs in a village meet to create a community council that will encourage new forms of cooperation among the town's clubs.
- Professors from several campuses meet to plan how they will run a two-month teaching program in the summer.
- Citizens and scholars interested in rational use of medicines create a group to plan reports, organize a conference on the topic, and decide how to direct their findings to officers of medical schools and pharmaceutical firms.
- Users of a newly purchased computer within a large organization meet to plan how they can best work with the machine and its staff.
- Neighbors gather to consider the value of a discussion group on topics of the day.
- Members of an advanced training course decide during their first session what they hope their meetings will cover and how.

These units had to solve the following sorts of questions. What kind of interests does each member have? How can we assist one another? Help the community? Who will do what? How can we best get superiors to listen to us? What is needed in our group's program? Who will assemble necessary information? Who will take the lead? Who can be members? Who will be excluded? What can we realistically expect to accomplish? These issues need to be answered for members to develop confidence in the ability of their group to reach its goals. They take us beyond the focus of our current concerns. We return to them in Chapter Eight.

Confidence in the ability of a group to achieve its aims may grow only gradually among members and leaders. The development of support for Martin Luther is a case in point. As a young priest and a professor of theology, he developed a distaste for the behavior of officials in the Catholic church after reading the writings of Wycliff and Huss and after observing the sale of indulgences within his own congregation. Both of the authors just mentioned deplored the ways funds were being used by the church and how this money was raised by priests. These practices, the writers believed, served purposes other than those on which the church was founded. Luther, a student of such matters but not a reformer, made a list of ninety-five complaints about things being done in the church, posted this set on the door of the local cathedral, and invited discussion of these topics at a local meeting; anyone was welcome. Luther was surprised by the number of persons who attended the forum and by the strong feelings they expressed, similar to his own. The discussants revealed more dissatisfaction than he had expected, and they urged him to act in ways he was not prepared for. He was frightened by what he had instigated and in following weeks held no more conferences.

Luther's unfavorable views about the behavior of his superiors persisted, however, and he continued to put his feelings in writing and to circulate these essays. Eventually he was brought to trial by civil authorities (his deviant religious behavior was a civil crime), accused of heresy, and given time to mend his ways, or else. Instead, he hid in disguise for months, wrote, and met with a few friends who gave him increasing encouragement for his beliefs. After a time, he recognized that his disaffection was too great, his desire to change matters too strong, and the understanding of his colleagues too reassuring for him to remain longer in a quiet place. Because he valued the help and support associates were offering him, he returned to public life and assembled a council of advisors. The actions of this group grew increasingly militant and eventually had the effects we all know.

Given that many groups are organized each year, it is surprising how little has been written on a general theory of organizing. There are books on how to create entities in specific fields; these include creating citizen-action bodies (Ross, 1973), "struggling" to achieve social change (the OM Collective, 1971), or controlling risks to the environment (Douglas and

Wildavsky, 1982). However, no volumes present a common set of steps to be used in forming units of all kinds.

4. *Conditions in their community encourage persons to establish a unit and to take part in its activities.* In addition to the trigger conditions we have been considering, groups are likely to be formed if developers and members are encouraged to do so. We can call conditions that supply this encouragement *promoters.* These promoters make creation of a unit easier. The way of life among individuals, for instance, makes them more or less ready to form groups. Persons more often create and join an entity if they live in the same neighborhood and share the same sidewalk, entrance door, or mailbox area (Festinger, Schachter, Back, 1950). Individuals from a given office, courtyard, church, pub, or club are more commonly found in the same organization than people who seldom see each other outside that unit. Chester Barnard (1938) observes that a group comes into being when individuals (a) are able to communicate with each other easily, (b) are willing to contribute to joint action, and (c) have a common purpose.

Even though frequent contacts among persons increase their chances of becoming a unit, some individuals are not attracted to being a member of any group, ever, and would rather work alone, come what may. I once asked students of varying ages (high school and college) whether they preferred to work for themselves alone or for the good of a group on each of a number of tasks that could be performed equally well alone or together. Two-thirds of the respondents said they would rather work alone and only one-third preferred to work for a group. Subjects who feared failure, and older students too, were most likely to favor working in a group (Zander, 1971). The possibility that there is an enduring personal disposition either to approach group membership or to avoid it warrants further study. Surely, where persons are more inclined to belong to an organization, they will more quickly form and more steadily maintain a group when that appears to be wise. Some writers (Mancur Olson, 1971, is one) believe that humans never join a group unless the benefits therefrom exceed the costs or unless they are coerced into membership by powerful others. If groups do not reward members, Olson says, these entities will disappear. Persons who can get the benefits of a group without incurring the costs of joining it become "free riders," living off the benefits it provides but never going near the body itself.

Often a group must be created by law to supplement a body that already exists. A public corporation must have a board of directors, a school system requires a set of trustees, and a university is to have a committee of professors who rule on the use of human beings as subjects in research on that campus. Laws also limit the aims and actions of public bodies, such as churches, banks, unions, cooperatives, or partnerships. And larger collectives operate through units they help local citizens create: franchises for fast foods, chapters of a fraternal order, regional agencies to evaluate the effects of industry on the environment, service clubs, or patriotic societies.

Research by social psychologists on the formation of groups has often examined why strangers become attracted to associate with one another—why they like one another. Do birds of a feather flock together? Or does like prefer unlike? Do the needy prefer the compassionate? These matters are discussed elsewhere by Berscheid and Walster (1978), Kanter (1972), Shaw (1981), and Zander (1982). Generally speaking, similar persons tend to come together more readily. As an illustration, Newcomb (1961) spent a two-year period monitoring the formation of subgroups within larger sets of college students in a rooming house. He was interested in the characteristics of young men who become close companions and of those who avoid one another. The most telling property of people who formed a cordial subset was similarity in their basic values, common beliefs about what behavior is right or wrong. Scott (1965) duplicated these results in a study of new members in five fraternities and five sororities at a university. Is this similarity of values as influential among employees in a workplace as it is among college students? Probably so, especially where values are salient to the work being done (among professionals for example) and participants believe there is a right and wrong way to do things. According to Tajfel (1970), it does not take much to make a number of people believe they constitute a group and that their unit is very different from other bodies. All it took, in

some of his studies, was to tell a set of strangers that they were
a group or would be one soon. Once they knew this simple fact,
their feelings toward outsiders or members of other groups became more negative than they had been. The strength of a new
group may be increased and confidence in its activities aroused
among members if persons in the unit have easy contact with
one another and are similar in their views and if the members
desire to remain as members (Zander, 1982).

Customs in a specific place or time generate kinds of
bodies that are not seen elsewhere. Examples are groups for discussing philosophy among ordinary citizens in ancient Greece,
heretical sects in early days of Christianity, posses to hunt
thieves in the early American West, groups for political indoc-
trination in the neighborhoods of Mao's China, discussions
among Japanese workers to improve the quality of their output,
voluntary amateur crews to rescue shipwrecked sailors off the
coasts of Norway, and guerrilla bands to battle better-equipped
armies in Yugoslavia, Cuba, Viet Nam, Cambodia, Afghanistan,
El Salvador, and Nicaragua.

Groups are more likely to appear if certain favorable
background circumstances exist. Scott (1981) has noted a number of promoters that may be present in a society:

- A high proportion of the population can read print.
- A high proportion have special training.
- Most of the populace live in cities.
- The citizens have an active social life.
- The people use money for barter and as a reward for services
  rendered.
- Some political unrest exists.
- Members of the society differ over its priorities.
- People compete with one another for resources.
- There are complex roles in the society.
- There are complex institutions in the society.
- Positions are won on merit, not on favoritism or on less sali-
  ent personal qualities.

The strong faith in the value of group membership in Japan is based on centuries of practice these people have had in

solving problems and living cooperatively in independent and small communities. Years ago, most people lived in isolated villages in the bottoms of small valleys. Government at the village level was conducted by an informal council to which each family sent a representative. This council established methods for netting fish in the river, cutting wood on the mountainsides, building dry roads through the paddies, operating schools, maintaining the local cemetery, and dealing with the flow of the valley's water when irrigating fields of rice. The council helped citizens collaborate on matters that affected all of them. The success of their joint plans was more important than the success of any individual's schemes because the needs of the whole community had to come first.

The procedures and attitudes neighbors developed in the governing of their villages were easily transferred to the operation of other kinds of organizations because managers, who themselves had been raised in villages, believed in the ability of workers to solve their joint problems through meetings and discussion. Thus it was natural that officers in a larger organization would invite workers to discuss dilemmas in that body, just as villagers had been doing for generations.

Customs concerning how Japanese would treat one another as persons were defined through their experience in groups, and these ways enhanced, in turn, the effectiveness and harmony of their organizations. Today, in a larger body (say, a factory), some small unit—not a person—is the prime part of the organization, and each of these teams is assigned a set of duties to be divided among participants according to members' preferences. There are no definitions of individual jobs such as those found in Western nations. Each member, furthermore, is expected to know all tasks in the team's assignment because division of labor among participants is flexible and frequently changes. The group as a whole (not each separate member) gets feedback on the quality of its work. Moreover, the Japanese have a number of methods for making group decisions in impersonal ways that do not require face-to-face interaction so that participants in a conference cannot know who opposes them or whom one is contradicting; thus interpersonal harmony is preserved within the group. A meeting in Japan is a joint effort to find a mutually agreeable solution, not a debate or an effort to persuade. Participants are expected to control their emotions at all times and to be rational in their actions as group members. Mutual obligations and interpersonal ease are major values of the Japanese.

In the United States, groups are not as widespread as in Japan, but they are probably more frequent than in England, Norway, Italy, Libya, or Iran. The way of life in groups is also different in the United States than in Japan. An illustration of these differences is seen in Table 5, which summarizes qualities in Japanese and American working groups. These contrasts suggest that participation in groups may be more comfortable for Japanese than for Americans.

Generally speaking, Japanese work for their group's good whereas Americans work for their personal good. Japanese emphasize interpersonal obligations; Americans stress individual rights.

Promoters of group formation can be found in the words of wise men. Their ideas often express values as precious as religious beliefs. For example, Buddha once said, "Have you heard that Vajjians foregather often, and hold frequent public meetings of their clans? So long as the Vajjians gather thus often, and frequent the public meetings of their clan, so long may they be expected not to decline but to prosper" (Durant, 1935). Other prominent proponents of the values in working through groups include Charlemagne, Confucius, Jefferson, Locke, T. Roosevelt, Saint Paul, and Tiberius. The views of men such as these form the intellectual environment of those who plan groups today.

To illustrate, a number of savants of the eighteenth century discussed the virtues of a social contract they took to be the major basis of organized society. Their writings have had an impact far beyond their time. Funk (1982) provides quotations from theorists whose writings have been used to justify the creation of Western social institutions, especially those that function under established laws.

Hobbes introduced the idea of the social contract in the

Table 5. Qualities of Japanese and American Work Groups.

Japan	United States
1. Groups of workers solve their own problems.	1. Managers provide solutions for their workers and require obedience to these.
2. Workers monitor and control the quality of things they make.	2. Official inspectors watch for poor products made by subordinates.
3. Tasks to be done for the larger organization are assigned to groups within which they are informally divided among members.	3. A task is assigned to an individual who has been hired to do that job. This person *owns* that duty and a relevant title.
4. Members work hard for the group, not for themselves. They take more pride in their group's achievement than in their own.	4. Workers strive for their own success, not the group's success.
5. Meeting obligations toward colleagues is most important.	5. Satisfying one's personal rights is most important.
6. Members cooperate with associates and help them.	6. Members strive to do better than their associates.
7. Controversial topics, confrontations, or disagreements are avoided.	7. Conflict among members is encouraged, and, under certain conditions, is taken to be a good thing.
8. Persons in one's social environment bear responsibility for one's acts.	8. Individuals are solely responsible for their own behavior.
9. Members should not embarrass or hurt others even if they must conceal their feelings to avoid doing so.	9. Candidness about colleagues is most important, so it does not matter if frank comments hurt others' feelings.
10. Sincerity of purpose is more important than precision in speaking or writing.	10. Articulate and persuasive communication is more highly prized than sincerity.

Source: Adapted from Zander, 1983.

following way: "[The agreement] is a covenant of every man with every man, in such manner as if every man should say to every man, *'I authorize and give up my right of governing myself to this man, or to this assembly of men, on this condition,*

*that they give up their right to him, and authorize all his ac-
tions in like manner.'* This done, the multitude so united in one
person, is called a *commonwealth,* in Latin *civitas"* (Funk,
1982, p. 43).

Rousseau had similar ideas: "If, then, we take from the
social pact everything which is not essential to it, we shall find
it reduced to the following terms: 'each of us contributes to the
group his person and the powers which he wields as a person,
and we receive into the body politic each individual as forming
an indivisible part of the whole' " (Funk, 1982, p. 44).

Rousseau added: "Whoso would undertake to give institutions to a People must work with full consciousness that he
has set himself to change, as it were, the very stuff of human
nature; to transform each individual who, in isolation, is a complete but solitary whole, into a part of something greater than
himself, from which, in a sense, he derives his life and his being;
to substitute a communal and moral existence for the purely
physical and independent life with which we are all of us en-
dowed by nature" (Funk, 1982, p. 44).

And Rousseau once more: "As soon as the act of association becomes a reality, it substitutes for the person of each of
the contracting parties a moral and collective body made up of
as many members as the constituting assembly has votes, which
body receives from this very act of constitution its unity, its
dispersed *self,* and its will" (Funk, 1982, p. 46).

From Althusius: "An association is initiated and maintained by a covenant among the symbiotes setting forth their
common agreement about the necessary and useful purposes to
be served by the association, and the means appropriate to fulfill these purposes" (Funk, 1982, p. 48).

Finally, from Houriou: "The idea of the enterprise is the
object of the enterprise, for the enterprise has the object of real-
izing the idea. The idea is so truly the object of the enterprise
that the enterprise becomes objective and acquires a social indi-
viduality by means of and for the idea. For when the idea of the
enterprise is propagated in the memories of an indefinite number of individuals, it comes to live an objective life in their sub-
conscious" (Funk, 1982, p. 56).

Views such as these encourage the formation of groups, their purposes, and their style.

Summary

The presence of trigger states arouses individuals to work toward creating a group. Among these states are:

1. *Particular conditions are taken to be unsatisfactory or to suggest an opportunity for favorable change.* Potential organizers realize that a situation is not what it might be and that something ought to be done. Examples of such conditions are fear among would-be members, displeasure with activities of larger organizations, personal problems, difficulties faced by people in the community, a too-heavy physical task, unpleasant duties, opportunity for earning money, need for formalization of an existing informal set, desire to get ahead, grievances against superiors, separate interests among certain types of persons, or services needed by society.

2. *A more satisfactory state of affairs is conceived by organizers.* Not only is something seen to be wrong; group developers foresee how things could be improved. These better possibilities are often invented by one person or a few persons, and others are then invited to improve on the plan and to join its activities.

3. *Members believe they will achieve a satisfactory state of affairs.* The organizers' efforts will be empty unless they trust, and get members to accept, that the group's activities will create the desired end. The leaders of a group are responsible for building confidence in the organization. Often, they can do this best by making it possible for members to build their own faith in the group's fate.

4. *Conditions in their community encourage persons to establish a unit and to take part in its activities.* These conditions are called *promoters*. Persons are more likely to form a group if sources of influence foster such a move or, at the least, offer little resistance to it. Some of these circumstances include: frequent contact occurs among potential members, there is similarity among members, personal preference for working as a

member is stronger than for working alone, more benefits are available to members, legal requirements exist for the creation of a body, or the way of life in a given place encourages group activity.

Other promoters include: a high proportion of the population in a community can read print, much of the population lives in cities, some political unrest exists, people compete with one another for resources, and complex roles operate in the society. Groups are more pervasive and effective, then, in urban settings. Traditions among people also influence the formation of groups and the way these are used. Japan and the United States, to illustrate, have contrasting ways of employing groups. Japanese appear to work for the good of the group while Americans work for the good of the member. Ancient Greeks and French savants in the eighteenth century had much to do with the way Americans view organizations. We consider the impacts of values in Chapter Six.

Additional Readings

Newcomb, T. *The Acquaintance Process.* New York: Holt, Rinehart & Winston, 1961. A study of how strangers form sets of friends.

Stinchcombe, A. L. "Social Structure and Organizations." In J. March (ed.), *Handbook of Organizations.* Skokie, Ill.: Rand McNally, 1965. A review of conditions that foster the formation of groups.

Toch, H. *Social Psychology of Social Movements.* Indianapolis, Ind.: Bobbs-Merrill, 1965. The origins and effects of social movements.

Zander, A. *Making Groups Effective.* San Francisco: Jossey-Bass, 1982. "Creating a Strong Group" discusses how responsible members may increase the strength of a group.

FOUR

Characteristics
of Group Purposes
and Their Effects

Each objective of a group possesses properties of its own, such as clarity, power, or flexibility, and these affect how well members live up to the group's aim and how much satisfaction they derive from efforts to attain that end. Under certain circumstances, certain characteristics of group purposes are probably better than others. Christopher (1974) proposes, for example, that the goodness of a company's goals depends on how directly the goals affect the work of individuals and groups, how well the targets are accepted by persons throughout the firm, how achievable they are, how well progress can be measured when advancing toward them, and how well members' actions are guided by them.

An organizer of a group or a manager of an established unit would be wise to make sure that the purposes of that organization have appropriate characteristics (properties) because improper ones make a group less effective.

Although we have few objective facts about the properties of group purposes, here is what some of them might be like when they are more fully examined.

Measurability of the Purpose

The measurability of a group's purpose is how reliably the actual attainment of a group's objective can be determined. A measurable objective indicates exactly what should change and how much if the end is to be considered achieved, and what events are to be accepted as evidence that the goal has in fact been reached. An immeasurable goal is an ambiguous criterion of achievement.

Often a group's purpose is phrased in obscure language that makes it difficult for members to know how much the unit has moved toward or away from that aim. For example, a club in a small town intends to "improve the culture of the community." The group therefore sponsors violin recitals, talks on art, and excursions to museums in a distant city. Do these programs improve the culture? How can members be sure?

Rotary International, a male service club, has the following purpose:

> The object of Rotary is to encourage and foster the ideal of service as a basis of worthy enterprise and, in particular, to encourage and foster:
> *First.* The development of acquaintance as an opportunity for service;
> *Second.* High ethical standards in business and professions; the recognition of the worthiness of all useful occupations, and the dignifying by each Rotarian of his occupation as an opportunity to serve society;
> *Third.* The application of the ideal of service by every Rotarian to his personal, business, and community life;
> *Fourth.* The advancement of international understanding, goodwill, and peace through a world fellowship of business and professional men united in the ideal of service.

The purpose of the Community Club in Rossmoor, an adult community, is "to promote civic knowledge and appreciation of Rossmoor, and understanding of its plan of operation;

and to promote and support measures affecting its continuing success as an outstandingly attractive community." The purpose of Friends of the Earth is "to reduce the impact of human activity in the environment and to ensure that we as a species adopt policies which permit life in its varied and beautiful forms to continue." The Digital Company says, "Growth is not our principal goal. Our goal is to be a quality organization and do a quality job, which means that we will be proud of our work and our product for years to come. As we achieve quality, growth comes as a result."

The goals of other kinds of groups are expressed a bit more exactly, even quantitatively. The objective of the football team at the University of Michigan is to win its games. For each contest, the team and each individual member have goals in such matters as number of yards to be gained, tackles made, blocks carried out, points scored by an opposing team, passes completed, or first downs achieved. Planners for business firms set objectives for profits, share of market, speed of delivery, turnover of personnel, reserves of money, productivity per quarter, quality of service, or quality of product. A church aims for an increase in membership, improvement in attendance at Sunday services, more cash in the collection plate, reduction in the cost of utilities, or number of persons baptized, along with movement of members toward less tangible purposes described in the creed of that congregation.

These examples suggest that groups differ in the types of data members need when they determine whether their group has achieved its goal. A precisely stated purpose describes exactly what things should change, and in what way, as a result of reaching the group's objective so that misinterpretation about attainment of that end is precluded. A *measurable* purpose or goal, then, identifies what events are to be accepted as evidence that the objective has been reached. To measure the achievements of a football team, one counts the number of tackles, yards, or points made by each side during the game. To assess the degree of profit in a business, one obtains figures showing the differences between income and outgo of dollars. It is hard, however, although not impossible, to evaluate achievement of purposes for the Rotary Club or for Friends of the Earth because the events that are taken as fulfilling their objectives are not precisely enough defined. Greater measurability ensures more reliability when one is determining whether a group has reached its objective. Furthermore, a measurable goal describes what to evaluate and how to do so. It allows members to judge better how satisfactory a given group performance is— how close it is to being satisfying. Mager (1962, 1972) has described these matters well for classrooms.

Attainment of a group's goal generates among participants a sense of closure along with a loss of desire to exert more effort toward that end. Such closure is most likely to develop when the goal is measurable because then members are better able to ascertain if their group has, in fact, achieved its target. An unmeasurable objective, we have noted, does not prescribe what must be known in order to decide whether the group's goal has been reached. Thus members with an unmeasurable mission cannot see how closely their end point is being approached. Instead, they often count things that can readily be counted, regardless of whether these tallies have clear relevance to achieving the aim of that body. They observe, for example, the number of recruits, attendance at meetings, amount produced, projects completed, length of stories in the newspaper, and the like as indirect evidence about movement toward the group's purpose. The inclination to work toward and to measure attainment of surrogate (but clear) aims is a significant aspect of purposive behavior in groups. We return to this practice several times, especially in Chapters Six and Seven.

When a group's purpose is proposed, its measurability may be influenced by a number of factors. For one thing, an objective is an abstract idea that cannot always be stated precisely, regardless of the care taken in wording it, because the ideas in it do not invariably lend themselves to exact exposition. A group's purpose often must be put in just a few words so it can be included in a charter, pledge, publicity handout, or speech by an executive officer. Precision is difficult to achieve in a brief definition. As a result, the statement of a group's purpose is more often poetry than prose.

Etzioni (1975) distinguishes between *stated* and *actual* goals of an organization. Stated objectives are published for "public" or "front" purposes. They are phrased so they win the approval of members and outsiders. They do not, however, describe the condition the organization is really trying to realize because the true objectives often are hidden. Etzioni suggests that observers should look behind the published aims of a unit to see if the actual ends are different from the alleged ones. He reports the results of a study in which it was observed that staff members in various parts of a mental hospital sought to attain states distinctly different from those put forth by the hospital in literature describing its purposes. The actual targets, moreover, were more measurable than the published ones.

Some organizations deliberately put their purposes in vague terms because it is safer for them to do so. In a newly forming firm or agency, organizers recognize that they can be blamed by employees or clients if the body later does things that were not proposed in the original articles of incorporation. In order to prevent such complaints, those drafting the group's charter list any and all purposes the unit might conceivably ever develop, even though the body can realistically pursue only a few of these at any one time. A danger here is that articles of partnership are legal documents that eventually can be used in a suit alleging that the organization did not try to achieve certain initially agreed-on ends (Funk, 1982). Communes and utopias, according to Kanter (1972), intentionally state their purposes vaguely so members can conduct various activities under them and these programs can legitimately be changed if that becomes necessary because of shifts in opportunities available to it. Indefinite goals are sensible, moreover, when it is important that subunits of a large organization have the freedom to function autonomously, as do separate teaching departments in a university (Cohen and March, 1974; Kanter, 1972; Wieland, 1969).

A nebulous goal may be preferred by decision makers because discussion among them in order to reach a mutually acceptable description of a unit's purpose arouses more disagreement than is desirable (Gross, 1965). In such a case, an ideally worded purpose is one that allows all parties to believe their own personal preferences are covered in the final draft—an ambiguous goal can make such a claim credible. Goals may be deliberately vague if a group's organizers are cynical about the value of having a target at all; such organizers prefer empty phrases because they feel obliged to have an objective but do not want a demanding one.

A group's activities might intentionally be made meaningless for participants in order to make them realize they have no freedom in their choice of goals. In the *Gulag Archipelago,* prisoners are ordered to dig a hole in the frozen earth and are then told to fill it. They are given no purpose for these actions because their guards intend to degrade, tire, or intimidate them through this assignment.

A purpose may be inexactly stated in order that it not unduly constrain the behavior of members. Collectives that encourage learning or creativity of participants typically have such a goal. Members might be engaged in activities such as group psychotherapy, research, art, writing, music, or dance. In these instances, the purpose of the group is to develop an atmosphere in which each individual may be as creative as desired, knowing that colleagues are available when needed, either as an audience for observing the finished work or as advisors during its composition. The group's purpose is to provide a supportive means, not an end.

The purpose of a group may intentionally be put in obscure language because it serves as a cover-up or excuse for activities that are not acceptable to persons in or outside the unit. A political party publishes an unpopular purpose in attractive phrases in order to win approval and votes. Terrorists declare that their robbery of a bank is to finance work toward laudable political aims. An unmeasurable purpose is said to be acceptable because activities toward that end are clearly valuable in their own right. A monthly potluck dinner attended by married couples, for instance, needs no justification beyond the fun and friendship involved. Members of a square-dance club view their evenings together as pleasurable events that place few demands on participants. If the club decides, however, to compete with other clubs in a statewide contest, a different intention arises for the club's sessions, and it now performs with precision and vigor so that the dancers might become skilled enough to win. Fun is set aside in favor of work.

Even though there can be advantages in unmeasurable goals and members frequently are pressed to establish such aims for their groups, we assume that decision makers most often prefer measurable ones. The reasons for these choices are discussed in Chapter Seven.

In contrast to the foregoing, if an organization is subject to special public laws, as is a business partnership, corporation, labor union, school, church, or cooperative, it is required under regulation to state its purpose precisely in the original charter of the group (Funk, 1982). In addition, as a way of indicating their degree of responsibility for events in each of several bodies, members of a newly organized body may be made to state their financial commitment to this unit compared with their commitment to other organizations. Both the groups and the members must make their intentions visible, then, at the outset of their organizing if they are legally limited in their objectives and activities.

The purposes of a body are often more clear to persons in one part of an organization than to those in another part. Organizers who invent a group's goal, assemble its members, or rise to central positions in the group are more likely to desire measurable objectives than are participants in peripheral roles. An officer of a club recalls its objectives more accurately than does a raw recruit. A director of a research project describes the theoretical problem the project staff is working on more precisely than the research assistant does. A minister makes more sense of the congregation's goals than does the president of the lay persons' society in that church.

Apparently, better managers push harder for more precise aims. Vaill (1982) compared high-performing and low-performing organizations. He observed that better units, compared with worse ones, had clearer purposes, leaders who worked harder to ensure that the goals were understood by members, and managers who were more favorable toward the purposes of the group.

Accessibility of the Purpose

The *accessibility* of a group's purpose describes whether specified activities in a group serve to move it toward attainment of its objectives. The degree of accessibility in a purpose is determined by the perceived probability that paths toward the goal will conduct the organization to its target. Accessibility is estimated by observing whether particular programs, projects, procedures, or policies of a group take it to its goal. This movement may be through psychological space, as in the solution of an intellectual problem and a change in beliefs. Or it might be through physical space, as in completing an overland journey, a construction job, or a product on an assembly line. Not all activities in a group are relevant to reaching its goal. The more appropriate they are (see Chapter Nine) and the more they make it possible to attain the goal, the more the goal has accessibility. A T-maze for a rat has perfect accessibility because there is a particular path that takes the rodent directly into the goal box. A clinic's attempt to test a new medicine has unknown accessibility at the outset of the trial and either high or low accessibility at the end, depending on how good the medicine turns out to be as a form of therapy for the illness it is supposed to cure.

Measurability and accessibility are related but independent concepts. Attainment of a goal may be measurable, but the best way to get there may not be known. Or a good path to a goal may be identified, but how to measure its attainment is not. This latter condition—accessible but unmeasurable—will not last long because evaluation of a path depends not only on understanding where members of the group want their unit to go but also on whether it has arrived. Once a method has led to development of a goal, it presumably can do so another time, and the goal has accessibility: means to achieve it are known; it can in fact be reached. Because the value of a potential path to a goal cannot be determined at all unless the goal is clear and its attainment can be measured, adequate measurability is a precursor to reasonable accessibility. A sensible goal is both measurable and accessible.

According to Van de Ven (1980), when a group's goals are not measurable or accessible, things happen in the group that are not favorable for it. In such a case, plans are confused, members have poorly defined duties, and they cannot tell what their organization is accomplishing. Unless the accessibility of a group's purpose is well laid out, moreover, responsibilities, methods, flow of work, channels of communication, and lines of authority become mixed up, and members' efforts do not move the body toward its goal. In an experimental study of the matters we are considering, Raven and Rietsema (1957) compared the consequences for members when, on the one hand, the goal and path to the goal were clear to participants and when, on the other hand, members did not fully understand the group's task or the procedure being followed to complete it. Comparing the effects of these experimental conditions, the researchers found that a member who had a more precise perception of the group's goal and of the path to that end was more interested in performing group-relevant duties, experienced greater feelings of group belongingness, and felt more empathy with the emotions of fellow members while they worked on the group's task. We note other consequences of goal measurability and accessibility in following chapters.

Importance of the Purpose

The importance of a group's purpose is shown by the size of the change it creates in properties of the group, in behavior of members, or in conditions in the unit's environment. These effects are engendered either by fulfillment of the group's ob-objective or by efforts to attain that end. The attention members give to a more important goal has a greater impact on more circumstances in and around the group. Synonyms for importance of a purpose are *size, range,* and *spread.* Ordinarily, members are aware of the significance of an important purpose and are favorably disposed toward attaining it. Important aims are more central to a group's existence whereas unimportant ones are peripheral in its life. Thus within a company, profit and share of market may be more important objectives than service to the community or adherence to local norms concerning the hiring of women or minority members. On a college football team, winning games and attracting large crowds is more important to those involved in that program than is ensuring that athletes get good grades or earn a degree from that school. Saving souls is more important in some churches than is collecting a full plate of cash on Sunday morning.

Power of the Purpose

The power of a group's purpose is the degree of influence that the purpose has on the behavior of group members. Because a group's purpose induces members to behave in particular ways, it can be conceived as an inducing agent, a source of influence. Objectives with greater power overcome more resistance in influencing members to fulfill them; ones with lesser power are less able to arouse members' actions toward the group's purpose. Since potent objectives have a stronger impact on behavior, they stimulate more interest in their achievement. The power and importance of a purpose may be closely correlated, but they are not alike in their impact on members.

Thomas and Zander (1959) report that a more powerful group objective (as revealed by how hard military personnel tried to reach a defined location during a trek lasting four days) had greater *instrumental value* to the men. This higher value was caused by members' estimates about two matters: (1) the chances that attainment of an immediate or proximate goal would ensure achievement of a more ultimate objective and (2) the amount of value members placed on attaining the more distant end. The immediate goal in this case was completion of the four-day hike toward the home base through deep snow without being caught by a search party. The hike was the final examination in a military training course on survival in a group emergency. The participants' ultimate goal was a promotion in rank based on the team's performance during the course and trek.

We might guess that the power of an immediate goal is greater if it is a challenge (but not too difficult), is measurable, is accepted by all members alike, provides feedback about the group's objective output, is supported by persons outside the unit, stimulates a stronger desire among members for the group to succeed, allows comparison with a rival group's attainment of its goal, and allows members to do well in the individual duties assigned to them (Zander, 1971).

Thibaut and Kelley (1959) propose that a group goal is a special instance of a group standard, which is a decision made by members about how they should act to help the group accomplish its purposes or maintain its existence. In accord with the approach of these writers, we expect that members will exert pressure on each other to conform to the requirements of the group's decision and reject those persons who do not conform to these demands (Cartwright and Zander, 1968). The power of a group over its members, it has been shown, is greater as the cohesiveness of the group is greater. Changes in a group's goal are therefore probably more difficult to bring about as the cohesiveness of the group becomes stronger (see Chapter Eight).

Intuition suggests that a group purpose might have more influence if, at one extreme, it had a stronger emotional appeal to participants or if, at the other, it were rationally sensible to them. An emotional impact may be a form of religious zeal, patriotic fervor, team spirit, or interpersonal fear. An aim based on responses such as these has a strong grip on those who share it. A rational impact of a goal is based on either its correctness as a solution to a problem facing the group or its appropriateness as a plan for future actions. We consider the affective and conative aspects of purposes when we examine how values and motives of members influence their choice of goals for their organization.

Flexibility of the Purpose

Flexibility is the degree to which a purpose will yield to change. Some purposes alter readily when decision makers set out to modify them; other objectives are more fixed. The alterations may be in the content of the goal or in properties we have been reviewing. Because purposes are at the heart of an organization, we take it for granted that purposes are more often rigid than pliable (to protect the integrity of the unit) and that special conditions are therefore necessary before changes in a group's aims can be made. Participants may recognize, for instance, that the difficulty of their group's goal ought to be changed to a harder or easier level, depending on whether the unit has succeeded or failed in reaching its target. Or managers may shift the group's goals because of a change in pertinent conditions that led to choosing the present target. Groups with flexible objectives include political parties, which revise their platform's planks as voting issues shift, and business firms, which take up new products as consumers' tastes move.

Members who cling closely to their unit's purposes often do so because their values would be transgressed by a modification or because they prize their group's success to date. A measurable, accessible, important, or influential goal is probably more inflexible than an unmeasurable, inaccessible, unimportant, or weak goal. This proposition is worthy of study.

Consonance of the Purpose

The consonance of a group's purpose is the degree to which that purpose fits with other purposes the group may have. More commonly than not, a group has several purposes, and some writers believe that this multiplicity is a good thing. Among these is Christopher (1974, p. 62), who wrote, "For every business, objectives are needed in every area in which performance and results vitally affect the success of the business. Objectives in terms of profit and sales volume are not enough." A set of several objectives can be valuable for a group if these are additive in their effect on members and thereby make movement toward each target more efficient. Multiple goals are useful, moreover, because they provide varied criteria for appraising the group's activities; thus members may "succeed" in some respects even though they "fail" in others. Any embarrassment because they have done poorly in certain matters is assuaged by their doing well in others. Discouragement is relieved by pride, and satisfaction is tempered by a realization that the group can yet be improved.

Scholars have noted that conflicting goals can cause unfavorable consequences for a group because members' moves toward one aim interfere with moves toward a different one. A firm, for example, may not be able to improve its product without decreasing the dividends it pays to shareholders. Nor can it press for greater productivity while decreasing the size of its work force (Seashore, 1965). Very likely, simultaneous efforts to move toward conflicting objectives reduce the effectiveness of a group, but there is little evidence to support this hunch (Wallroth, 1968). Peters and Waterman (1982) report that more successful businesses appear to be more concerned about consistency in their objectives and that better firms have fewer objectives (or only one) and therefore tend to have less dissonance among their aims. An organization may have contrasting purposes because it adheres to conflicting values, such as creativity versus strict rules, decentralized control versus centralized administration, or big growth versus big dividends.

When an organization has several objectives, different members may have different preferences among these, and this leads to incongruency in actors' efforts to attain their aims. Because all goals cannot be simultaneously satisfied, managers of a group must choose which to stress and which to pass by for the moment. Conflicts within a group caused by members working toward contrasting goals can be prevented by giving each of the conflicting objectives to physically separated divisions of the organization, thereby keeping apart persons who have separate aims (Cyert and March, 1963). Or a group's officers may take up rival goals sequentially or even allow subunits to go different ways as long as their activities do not cause mutual interference (Wallroth, 1968). The accomplishment of some goals provides a means for the achievement of others; one cannot attain the second without accomplishing the first. In such a series, sometimes called a *hierarchy of goals,* efficient work toward one objective speeds the completing of others if they are taken up in the proper sequence.

Cooperativeness of the Purpose

The cooperativeness of a group's purpose is the degree to which each member's gain is contingent on the group's output but independent of personal score. In certain groups, members earn special benefits. An example is a business firm that pays more to an employee who produces more or pays a commission whenever an employee makes a sale. In a *cooperative* goal, each member gets an equal share of what the group earns as a whole. Thus a participant benefits whenever any member makes a contribution to the group's total actions. And because each member's individual score has no direct bearing on personal rewards, members are willing to sacrifice their own efforts and scores in the interest of the group's performance. When this kind of goal is present, members appreciate what others do for the group, encourage and praise others' efforts, and expend their own energy in behalf of the organization's good. A *competitive* goal is one in which each member receives a reward independent of the group's output and contingent only on that member's own separate score. The more points members make as individuals, the more gain they make. This system of compensation provides members with an incentive to increase their own tallies, regardless of its good or bad effect on the group, and to prevent or decrease the scores of other members whenever possible. When this kind of goal is present, members do not appreciate a good performance by a rival and work primarily in behalf of their own personal good (Deutsch, 1949).

Difficulty of the Purpose

The difficulty of a group's purpose is determined by the amount of energy, ability, time, or resources required to achieve that purpose. The goals members of a group consider when choosing its objectives may be arrayed along a scale of difficulty from easy to hard. More difficult goals require more energy, resources, time, or ability of members. When participants in a group select a given goal and try to attain it, they learn that their group can reach certain scores more easily than others. Members' *perceived* probability of success by their group is their judgment of the likelihood that the unit will successfully reach a given level of excellence when it tries to do so. Such a perceived probability will be smaller for a difficult score and larger for an easier one.

We distinguish between an objective measure and a subjective one for ordering the difficulty of group goals. Objective scores are measured in the minutes and seconds a mile relay team takes to complete a race, the number of slippers an assembly line completes in a day, or the number of weeks needed to construct a bridge. This objective concept of difficulty requires that the goal be reasonably measurable and accessible. A subjective estimate is a guess about how difficult each degree of accomplishment (level of goal) will be for a given group in the light of its resources and accomplishments. What is hard for one crew may be easy for another. Thus one group sets a harder or easier subjective goal than others. How this happens and why is discussed in Chapter Seven.

If responsible members are to set a sensible goal for their group, they need to have evidence about how well the unit performs in attempts to reach one goal or another. Clearly, they can get information of this kind only if members know when they have completed a given goal, or when they have failed to do so, and by how much. Thus we can judge the difficulty of a group's objective more rationally if it is more measurable and accessible.

Additional properties of a group have consequences for its way of life. We can only mention these. They include the strategy or tactics needed for reaching the goal, its time depth, its timeliness, its complexity, its acceptability to members, and its linkage to other objectives (that is, its position in a series when each must be completed in the proper order).

Members' Preferences for Particular Properties

Members prefer particular properties of purposes when the participants think these characteristics make their group's objective more useful. Members probably favor, as we have already suggested, that the power of a purpose be strong rather than weak, measurable rather than immeasurable, and accessible rather than inaccessible. Furthermore, persons in a unit want its goal to be important rather than unimportant. This preference is perhaps more likely to develop if the goal is transitive (directed toward persons beyond the boundary of the unit) than if it is reflexive (directed toward the inside of the unit). A group's purpose is probably more important to a local board of education, say, than to a poetry reading society. The central administration committee of a firm has more important purposes than the crew in charge of buildings and grounds.

Members often value a flexible objective more than an inflexible one. This choice occurs, we suppose, because its greater changeability means that it can be improved when that is necessary, thereby maintaining maximal usefulness for members. A purpose, in contrast, may be inflexible and derive its strength from its agreement with an established dogma (as in a religious organization), or with a revered constitution in a club, company, or governing body.

Members choose consonant purposes more than contradictory ones because the former have a harmonious and additive effect, each supplementing the other, whereas the latter create interpersonal strain and conflict among aims, each weakening the other. Finally, members want a challenging goal—one a bit harder than those their group has already achieved—instead of a goal that is very easy or very hard. We consider the reasons for this preference in Chapters Seven and Eight when we examine how members' desires for group achievement determine the goal they want for their group.

Summary

The impact of a group's purpose depends not only on its substantive content but also on its characteristics, which include the following:

• The measurability of a group's purpose denotes the degree of precision possible when determining whether a group has fulfilled its aim. A measurable objective exactly describes what should change in the group, and to what extent, if one is to say that the intent of the unit has been achieved. An unmeasurable purpose is so vaguely worded that one cannot tell reliably whether the group has accomplished its mission.

- The accessibility of a group's purpose is the degree of confidence among members that particular activities will bring about a consequence they desire. An accessible goal can be reached in known ways. An inaccessible goal has no designated path toward its attainment.
- The importance of a group's purpose is shown by the number of conditions within and outside the group that are affected by members' efforts to attain the group's goal. It is a subjective judgment based on how members evaluate the effectiveness of their group's efforts. An unimportant goal generates few consequences for events within the group.
- The power of a group's purpose is its capacity to change the behavior of members in a particular way. A more powerful objective places stronger demands on members to fulfill its requirements. A weaker one arouses little effort by members to achieve it.
- The flexibility of a group's purpose indicates how readily it can be altered. A flexible mission is one that members can easily change when a shift appears wise. A rigid one is firm against efforts to shift it.
- The consonance of a group's purpose is the degree of fit among several group aims. Consonant purposes can be additive in their effects on members' behavior and can provide multiple criteria for success in a group. Dissonant purposes generate conflict among members or emphasize one aim at the expense of others.
- The cooperativeness of a group's purpose is the degree to which it inspires members to help one another toward an outcome that is beneficial for the group as a whole. Each member's gain is an equal share of the group's production. Under a competitive purpose, each member works for his own benefit, not for the good of colleagues or the group as a whole.
- The difficulty of a group's purpose, in objective terms, is the amount of effort or resources required to accomplish it. The difficulty of a purpose in subjective terms is described by the members' perceived probability of success; that is, by their judgment of the likelihood that the unit will

reach a given quality of performance when members try to do so.

Because the consequences of these properties are more desirable to some people than to others, members in a given group prefer group objectives with particular properties or combinations of properties. The presence of preferred characteristics makes the purpose more useful to some members or to the group as a unit.

Additional Readings

Etzioni, A. *A Comparative Analysis of Complex Organizations.* New York: Free Press, 1975. Discusses the qualities of overt and covert purposes in organizations.

Kets de Vries, M. F. R., and Miller, D. *The Neurotic Organization: Diagnosing and Changing Counterproductive Styles of Management.* San Francisco: Jossey-Bass, 1984. Attributes of an organization reflect the personalities of influential officers.

Mager, R. F. *Preparing Instructional Objectives.* Belmont, Calif.: Pitman Learning, 1962. A manual for teachers on how to identify measurable objectives for the classroom.

Wallroth, C. "An Analysis of Means-End Structure." *Acta Sociologica,* 1968, *11,* 110–118. How multiple goals cause problems for an organization.

Warriner, C. K. "The Problem of Organizational Purposes." *Sociological Quarterly,* 1965, *6,* 139–146. How to detect the most influential goals in an organization.

FIVE

Defining
Appropriate Purposes

A group is organized, we are assuming, if the leader (or others) is not satisfied with a situation, conceives of a better state of affairs, and believes that a planned unit can generate this improved condition. This better state is the group's purpose—a property a group must have if it is to attract members both at a group's beginning and later. Members' approval of the unit's objective will be stronger if the target conforms to their values and suits their motives.

Those who belong to a group want their unit to have a purpose. They become uncertain and uncomfortable if it has no declared end state, because members then have no basis for knowing why certain things are expected of them in that unit and why colleagues do what they do (Locke, 1968; Raven and Rietsema, 1957; Vaill, 1982; Feather, 1982). In such cases, confusion appears to dominate the group's activities. In the absence of a group's purpose, members cannot predict the course of future actions in that body and cannot sensibly prepare for them. They ask themselves if their personal goals can be achieved inside that unit. Will their services be useful to the organization? What degree of similarity is there between their own goals and those of the total body? How will performance be evaluated by colleagues? Is it possible to get ahead in the organization?

Will they recognize how to help colleagues in their efforts? Will they realize what activities the group ought to sponsor? Can they identify a success or a failure by the body? Uncertain answers to queries such as these make members unsure about their role in the body. This uncertainty is probably stronger in a workplace than in a more relaxed setting and in an achievement-oriented society, such as Japan, Israel, or the United States, than in India, Russia, or the Philippines, where citizens are less concerned about accomplishments. Uneasiness may not develop among participants in a group that has no clear purpose if that organization exists to help each individual do what he or she separately wishes, as in a studio, convalescent hospital, or research institute where participants are encouraged to seek separate aims.

All in all, a member is not able to prefer a course for an organization and cannot evaluate the usefulness of activities by colleagues in that unit, unless there is a criterion to use as a base line in assessing these performances. A group's purpose is such a criterion. It goes without saying that a member who wishes to stimulate purposeful, group-oriented efforts among colleagues can better arouse this involvement by pointing out to them the value of their group's objective—the kind of satisfaction members will have when it is attained (see Chapter Seven).

Karl Weick (1979) observes that members in many groups prefer to act first and to find a justification (a purpose) for their actions later on. In such a case, a group's purpose is retrospective, not prospective. This purpose may be obscure or nebulous for reasons we have noted. Weick holds that most purposes of groups are vague and weak and do not have a vital part in the group's way of life. Often, this is true. But is a weak purpose always a useless one? We return to Weick's views in a few pages.

A person who is developing a group may conceive of how a situation could be improved but may not be able to define a unit's purpose precisely enough so that participants can use it as a guide for action. The chances are good, moreover, that the developer will be bound to put the group's purpose in ambiguous terms if the goal is for participants to support an abstract concept, such as freedom of speech, love of country, ways of salvation, improvement in personal health, or artistic appreciation. Or the developer intentionally might not reveal to members the end state he or she privately has in mind. If the group's purpose is expressed precisely participants may not accept it because they are not able to do much toward that end. In each of these instances, a purpose exists for a group but it is not compelling for members.

Even when organizers succeed in defining a group's purpose exactly, this objective is not always used as a guide for activities in that body (see Chapter Eight). Warriner (1965) and Etzioni (1975) contend that the stated purpose of an organization is frequently a false facade and that anyone who wants to know its true objective should look at what members are actually doing. Warriner proposes that one can better determine a unit's purpose by noting the functions members perform for that body (rolling bandages, making music, collecting funds, hauling in nets of fish), rank-ordering these functions in accord with their apparent value for the group, and observing how much time members spend on each activity. The programs with the most value, the ones that have the most time devoted to them, are taken to be the group's prime purposes, regardless of whether they are mentioned when members describe objectives of their entity.

Cohen and March (1974) aver that the procedure proposed by Warriner for separating a real purpose from a professed one is not a wise way for an outsider to identify the true aim of an organization because the results of such an inquiry usually fail several questions: Is the "true" purpose uniquely consistent with behavior? Does it produce that behavior? Could the professed purpose also cause those actions? Is the purpose stable? And is it a reliable predictor of behavior? These are stringent demands. The objective of many quite viable groups cannot meet such criteria.

Does a group have a purpose if the person who forms the body has an objective in mind but does not tell members about it or interest members in it? What if individuals are assigned to membership and are given a mission by the one who selects them to be members? Is this directed objective the property of members? Do voluntary participants grasp goals more firmly than members who are required to join? And does a group have a purpose if it has an aim that members ignore, even though it is in the by-laws for the organization? What does it mean, in short, for a group to *have* a purpose? A group possesses a purpose, we propose, if either of the following two circumstances are present. First, if the executive officers of a unit define a purpose for it and successfully guide the activities of members in accord with that objective, whether or not the officials require members to develop full commitment to this goal. Second, a group has a purpose if members agree on one for the unit through a decision-making process in which participants compare their preferred purposes for the group and choose among these. A purpose, it is clear, can be pressed upon members, created by their group through members' decision making, or both. In either case, it is important that members accept the purpose to some degree and behave in ways that are in accord with that aim. It is not enough to have an objective described in the by-laws if members ignore it as a guide to behavior. Where such a situation exists, members soon invent other ends they can value and attain. More on this in a moment.

Importance of Having a Group Purpose

Members become increasingly concerned that their group have a purpose if the assembled persons are, in fact, obviously a group. A collection of individuals constitutes such a body to a greater degree as they have more interaction and as they become more dependent on one another in their activities within that unit. Thus participants will more strongly want a joint purpose when events enhance their amount of interaction and interdependence. In contrast, the desire for a jointly shared objective is minimized if persons work on an activity (for example, picking apples from trees) that causes them to have little interaction or interdependence.

A second circumstance that makes members eager to have a group purpose is their recognition that absence of a joint objective (in respect to some matter that interests them) is threatening to cause bad consequences for the group's existence. Participants may be competing member against member, for instance, and this rivalry pushes each to work primarily for personal gains and to block any benefits for rivals. Or there is frequent conflict among colleagues caused by contrasts in their goals, and this clash of interests generates unpleasant relations among them. Persons with dissimilar intentions move in separate directions and, when constrained to work in proximity, get in one another's way. In such cases, members lose interest in the group, ask for transfers from it, or do not do their jobs well. Participants become more relaxed about their need for a group purpose, in contrast, if they are cooperating, thinking alike, following similar interests, collaborating easily, and remaining members of the body.

Third, the desire for a purpose becomes stronger when members foresee in the future increasingly unpleasant outcomes of the kind just cited. In summary, members of some groups have a greater desire for a group purpose, and the strength of this wish is reduced by desirable situations.

Effects of a Nebulous Purpose

Some kinds of groups (such as churches, political parties, service clubs, patriotic bodies, character-building associations, or schools) have purposes the attainment of which cannot be measured reliably (they are, in fact, immeasurable) and cannot be reached by designated means (they are inaccessible). Despite such vague purposes, these groups survive and prosper.

A broad purpose may be acceptable to members for reasons that have nothing to do with the group. The reasons may be local traditions, childhood experiences, ethnic values, or private ambitions. Membership in the group may also be seen as a means to attain personal goals (such as getting more clients, customers, patients, contracts, friends, or followers in the community), and a vague objective does not interfere with aims of that kind. Members may tolerate unclear group purposes because it pleases others. A woman attends a weekly coffee hour, where uninteresting ladies only exchange trivial gossip, because neighbors urge her to come along with them. A son goes to church reluctantly because doing so makes his mother happy. Members are assigned to a group by a powerful superior who expects them to do what they are told without being given a reason for these demands. In bodies with vague aims, the group's programs may become attractive to members, and completion of these may be a source of satisfaction—the initial purposes turn out to be, comparatively speaking, weaker sources of influence. In sum, obscure objectives are often tolerated because they justify the creation and maintenance of a group and members are either adequately satisfied with what goes on there or will live with unsatisfying ambiguity.

If members cannot tell whether their unit has accomplished its goal because it is immeasurable, they may, as we have remarked, set up more precise substitute goals whose attainment can be reliably measured. Thereafter, members are directed toward accomplishing these clearer ends (sometimes called subgoals), and the larger, vaguer, beginning purposes are maintained but overlooked in the day-to-day operations of the group. Such withdrawal of prior commitment to the unit's too obscure objectives has caused some scholars to assert that organizations do not have any purposes at all (Georgiou, 1973; Seashore and Yuchtman, 1966; Weick, 1979). These critics overlook that more precise goals can be created by members when the initial purposes in their group are too nebulous. The original objective may remain honored on the record but in reality be ignored in favor of an aim whose attainment is more measurable and accessible. Members thereafter place greater emphasis on the accomplishment of these clearer, substitute ends than on achievement of the original, imprecise purposes. As was observed earlier, these substitute goals may have no relevance to initial aims of the body. Because of their irrelevance, one can see persons in organizations that profess noble purposes (service, welfare, progress, salvation, withdrawal from society) working to achieve clearer but more minor ends (reducing scrap loss, controlling pollution, increasing number of graduates) while ignoring their laudable and abstract ends (see Chapter Nine).

Because a member who is interested in the fate of the group becomes uncomfortable if unsure the group can control events, that person may engage in aspects of the organization's

activities that are self-satisfying even though these do not help
the group accomplish its objectives. Such a member may seek
satisfaction of personal aims, for example, by having fun, making new friends, obtaining useful information, or enhancing personal status in the community. Another member may see newly
developed qualities of the group as sources of satisfaction:
growing in numbers, providing a benefit for bystanders, or creating security for members.

People cope with vague group objectives in other ways.
They may reduce their part in the unit by being absent from it,
doing less for it, or drifting into marginal membership. They
may suggest that the group be dissolved and help in that disso-
lution. But anyone who recalls how well useless groups survive,
even when members are tired of them, knows that abolishment
of a group is difficult. Members may move to a different organization where purposes are measurable and accessible. Or they
may develop a rival unit containing characteristics that were
missing in the one they left.

Planning for a Group's Purpose

In contrast to how most living entities are conceived, a
group is not given birth unless there is a purpose in mind for it.
A developer will not fabricate a body without a reason for
doing so, and members will not lay out a group's course without an aim. In what follows, we consider the origin of a group's
objective as the group is just being formed, when it is well
under way, and when its purpose is being modified and a new
one being put in place. Any decision for a group's operation, including a choice of its central purpose, requires that familiar
problem-solving steps be taken, as described by Janis (1972),
Janis and Mann (1977), or Zander (1982). Those most relevant
to choosing a purpose are now briefly noted.

Choosing Good Group Goals

Cohen and March (1974) assert that some organizations
have unwise purposes because the persons who create these
bodies do not employ their intuition or imagination effectively

when defining objectives. The authors assume that some aims are better than others and that a good end is more likely to be chosen if planners use methods that unleash their creativity. Cohen and March suggest means for such unleashing: A group's developers may find out what comparable bodies are planning to do, thereby helping themselves to identify overlooked alternatives and to judge how feasible these functions are for their own unit. Or a superordinate creating a subgroup requires subordinates to propose an objective for their new unit within a stated time limit; if they do not do this quickly enough, members are told, they will have to accept a goal set for them by the superior. A further procedure is to estimate how closely each proposed goal comes to an ideal that is impractical at the moment; closer is better. Another is to abandon efforts to make separate purposes consonant, recognizing that inconsistency among objectives is bound to occur, is a source of stimulation itself, and seldom does enduring harm.

Cohen and March suggest that managers of an established body can become more flexible in evaluating and selecting their group's objectives by experimenting with several methods. They may, for example, treat new purposes as hypotheses about the directions a group could pursue. These hypotheses are then tested, and the proposed objectives are later kept or abandoned as experience suggests. A different approach asks members to trust their intuition as a source of good ideas—because inventiveness is not always due to logical thinking. It is helpful, furthermore, for members to view a gap between group aim and outcome as the result of an exploratory trial from which a lesson can be learned rather than viewing it as a mistake. Also, those who plan for a group might best be skeptical about how things previously have been done there because good past practices can now be inadequate. Finally, experience in the group provides data that may be interpreted differently on separate occasions, depending on conditions outside the group. These writers urge us to look beyond mere rationality as we plan the direction of a group's activities.

William Christopher, in his book *The Achieving Enterprise* (1974), describes how members of a business firm might choose a purpose for their organization. The groups he discusses are in operation and already have an aim, and members wish to evaluate, clarify, or replace that aim. In order to make these moves wisely, Christopher proposes that decision makers first define the *identity* of their unit. An identity, as he sees it, is contained in members' answers to two central questions: What are we? What shall we become? Or, more exactly, What is this group? What should it become?

Although Christopher does not provide a conceptual definition of the term *identity*, he clearly believes that it is a basis for a group's objective. He says, for instance, that without an identity "there will be too many random actions, too many problems, too many roads to travel, too many emergencies, too many projects, too many opportunities" (p. 34). An identity for a group allows deciders to determine what the body should try to achieve. Answers to the two identity questions might be reached by discussion among persons in a small group of individuals from the larger body. Through this interaction, they develop ideas they might not have crafted during private thought. These ideas can be supplemented by advice from colleagues, community councils, customers, or consultants. Additional thoughts may be obtained from publications in engineering, economics, consumer preferences, history of civilization, current events, ethical guidelines, or successes of rival groups.

Christopher recommends that discussants first prepare relevant facts about their organization through conducting what he calls an *audit*. An audit consists of answers to a list of questions about the unit's resources and products. This line of questioning in a business firm, according to Christopher, might take up issues such as the following.

- What are our product lines?
- What are the major products for each line?
- Who are our major competitors?
- Where are our best opportunities over the next few years?
- What are our technical strengths?
- What are our major problem areas?
- What are our financial resources?
- What changes or new areas of operation might we consider?
- What areas of concentration are most promising for us?

When responses to such queries are in hand, members use these as basic information for their work on the fundamental issues: What are we? What should we become? These topics are discussed separately for the organization as a whole, for each department, and for individuals. Christopher suggests that replies to the two issues be ordered under five headings:

1. Products and services provided by the organization
2. Persons or groups served by the organization
3. Available competence of members in technical, marketing, financial, entrepreneurial, or research matters
4. Resources available to the unit in facilities or capital
5. The geographical area served by the organization

Ideas placed under these five categories describe what the group is now. Then a discussion of how these ought to be changed generates ideas for potential achievements—for what the group ought to become. Defining a group's identity presses members to favor goals in accord with that definition. According to Christopher, members tend to set group goals in one or more of the following areas of performance originally described by Drucker (1954): market standing, innovation, productivity, physical and financial resources, profitability, manager performance, manager development, worker performance, and attitude and responsibility of employees. Each of these areas should be discussed by members, in response to a lead-in question such as the following: In consideration of our concept of identity, what are we and what do we wish to become; and guided by our business intelligence, what are the most important objectives for us, at this time, in the key performance area of _____? A discussion of responses to this question produces a number of potential objectives. Members then choose the ones that are most likely to be significant.

Christopher gives examples of objectives by describing how a business sought to continue as a forerunner in its field through creating and selling a new product. Members of the company accordingly set several specific goals.

1. Maintain or achieve a leading market share in the specific business areas targeted for concentration of effort and resources. [These are separately identified.]
2. By 197– double operating income with programs in place and successfully functioning to ensure continuing growth in profitability of 10% a year or more.
3. By internal development or by acquisition commercialize two or more new ventures prior to 197– that will: (a) enhance earnings in an existing business area or (b) enable the company to achieve a leading position in a new growth segment of the plastics industry. By the end of 197– commercialize one of those ventures and have programs for at least one more prepared.
4. Target and achieve experience-curve productivity improvements and thereby achieve favorably competitive costs in targeted business area segments.
5. Relate experience-curve economics to pricing and develop appropriate pricing strategies.
6. Conduct operations to meet the company's responsibilities to its employees, the general public, the communities in which it operates, and the requirements of applicable law.
7. Create a participative management environment within the company that can develop the talent, the will, and the group effectiveness to accomplish company goals [p. 57].

Each department in the firm then developed its own goals that, when accomplished, would help the total organization fulfill these aims. All levels in the hierarchy of the organization developed consonant goals in this way.

A group's purpose will be most useful if it is accepted by all members. Cyert and March (1963) note, however, that a group contains individuals who have diverse ideas about what the purpose of their group might be. In that case, it is not always easy for all members to come to a common view about their unit's purpose. Furthermore, separate participants may be exposed to different influences from outside the group, and these external pressures can increase current contrasts among members' ideas. Accordingly, a decision reached by members about the goal of their group may have a different meaning to some persons if the statement of the objective glosses over inter-member disagreement or uncertainty about the plan. Participants would be wise, Cyert and March propose, to recognize that a unit's purpose is not permanently fixed but can be evaluated, interpreted, or modified as members' experience grows in working with it. These authors contend that members tend to give most weight to their personal objectives, and when they accept a goal for the group, they retain reservations about that goal, honoring it only if there is a personal advantage in doing so. Each member assumes, moreover, that colleagues are also skeptical about the group's objective.

An objective of an organization, I believe, is not always the treaty among self-seeking rivals March and his colleagues take it to be. Perhaps members' lack of interest in their total group's purpose is more common in business firms (the type of organizations Cyert and March most often study) than in other kinds of entities. There can be no doubt, however, that in a good proportion of collectives, including companies, the goals of the group may be more important to a member than personal goals are. Think of how often a person puts the good of the group ahead of personal gain in a family, church, ship, team, military unit, acting troupe, shop, or factory (Zander, 1971). Among organizations created to make a profit, better firms pay more attention to creating organizational purposes, helping members see how important these purposes are, and getting support for the objectives of the body than they do to advancing personal gains of individual employees (Peters and Waterman, 1982).

H. Igor Ansoff (1965, p. 39), a student of strategies used by corporations in their daily operations, says, "Contrary to Cyert and March, we assume that the business firm does have objectives which are different and distinct from individual objectives of participants . . . objectives for a business firm can be inferred from its relationship to the environment, from its internal structure, from the functions it performs, and from its past history . . . we define an objective as a measure of the efficiency of the resource-conversion process. An objective contains three elements: the particular attribute that is chosen as a measure of efficiency, the yardstick or scale by which the attribute is measured, and the goal, the particular value on the scale which the firm seeks to attain." In Ansoff's view, the major attribute for a company is return on its equity, and its goal is to optimize this return. Subsidiary objectives are developed, and attainment of these is to help the unit reach its major objective. Ansoff proposes that ethical, esthetic, and economic values, along with the objectives observed in rival firms and what is favored in current business practice, are helpful when members are deciding what the purpose of a company (other than profit) is to be.

Achieving a Common Point of View

Frequently, the major problem in establishing a purpose for a group is that of achieving a common point of view, a consensus. In order to attain this unitary aim, members need to know what others think, have sufficient time to evaluate unfamiliar ideas, hear how colleagues feel, and learn how members respond to discussants' positions. Procedures such as these are fostered in the Delphi technique (Delbecq, Van de Ven, and Gustafson, 1975; Pfeiffer, 1968). We need research on how well this method leads to useful results.

The Delphi approach allows group decisions to be reached without holding a face-to-face meeting. All contacts among participants are made through messages to and from one central person. No participant knows who thinks what, and thus any discussant can offer unusual thoughts or opposition without fear of reprisal from colleagues. Before the decision process begins, it is necessary to determine who will run it and who will take part in the decision making. The best number of participants is between twenty and thirty persons. Too many makes the whole thing too cumbersome. Too few restricts the variety of ideas to be weighed. There are four steps in the process.

Step One. Each person who is to participate in the procedure is sent one question. For example:

> In the decade ahead, the Ajax Mirror Com-
> pany should concentrate its energies and resources
> on ——.

Each respondent is asked to provide *four to ten endings
to such a stem sentence.* Respondents are asked to put their
names on their papers and are told to whom the forms should
be returned.

These data are then arranged by the supervisor into separate categories that eliminate redundancy among remarks by
individuals. This arranged list is considerably shorter than the
original set of all responses. Examples of some items include:

- Lines of authority should be clarified and roles more ex-
  plicitly defined.
- New products must be added to our product line. What
  ones?
- Staff members should be helped to move up in the company by providing them with appropriate in-service training opportunities.
- Profit *über alles.*

Step Two. Each participant is provided a new question-
naire on which all the processed answers generated in step one
are listed. The respondent is told the following:

> After each of the following statements, indi-
> cate the priority you would attach to this activity.
> Use the following key:
> 1. Top priority
> 2. Second priority
> 3. Maintain action or service at present level
> 4. Reduce or discontinue action—do not ini-
>   tiate action in this area
> In order to help us be realistic about the limits on
> our resources, please distribute your priority rat-
> ings so that there is a fairly equal number of 1s,
> 2s, 3s, and 4s.

This forced distribution is important because it requires

respondents to give relatively lower priorities to some matters. Respondents are again asked to put their names on their papers.

Step Three. In this stage, the data are returned to each respondent once more, this time in such a way that the items in our example are again listed and the average priority rating derived in step two is given for each item. In addition, the subject's own previous priority rating is reproduced (this is possible because the respondents put their names on their papers). The participants are asked to compare their individual priorities with the average of the group, and if they wish, to give a new priority for any items.

Whenever a respondent provides a rating different from the average of the group, that person is also asked to state the reason for this variation as fully and clearly as possible.

Step Four. Now a new average priority for each item is reported to participants along with the reasons given by respondents who disagreed with the prior average. Respondents are again asked to give a rating on the basis of these newer data and to weigh the arguments advanced by those who did not agree with the consensus reached in step three. These ratings are again to be distributed as equally as possible. Often, it is found, members change their own ratings on the strength of the arguments offered by colleagues. It is important to note, however, that the content of the argument is in the foreground, not the status or the personality of the person presenting a given view. With the exception of the supervisor, no one knows who said what.

Following the fourth step, the data are collated into a report that lists all items in order of their average priority along with the arguments for each. This report is the final product of the Delphi procedure. It contains a summation of the views of members. In order to clear the air, a last step would be to hold a face-to-face meeting for discussion of the final report.

Some group purposes, perhaps a majority of better refined ones, are phrased only after members have begun acting together as a group and need a reason to account for what they are doing. Their initial actions, based on a broad and general aim, help them delineate some specific moves, just as a first draft helps a writer decide what he or she wants to say. As we noted earlier, this notion that a purpose may be a postsummary rather than a preplan has been vividly presented by Weick (1979). He assumes that (1) members begin interpersonal interaction while believing in *diverse goals* for the group, that (2) they collaborate at the outset through creating *common means* to help them work in coordination, which leads them (3) to agree on *common* and shared *goals*, and then to (4) *diverse means*, which lead once again to (1) *diverse goals* and so on. The cycle just described suggests that members' personal aims are best served within a group by employment of common means at the start rather than by first using common goals. Weick believes that ends need not be common among members in the beginning, but means need to be shared by them at the first so that participants will not interfere with each other's moves. Later on, members gradually shift from using only common means to delineating common aims, thereby ensuring that useful plans in the group are preserved for the future. They create rules and policies so that procedures will fulfill joint objectives and so that their activities will have a similar meaning among members. In short, participants act first and find a purpose for their actions later. Weick puts it this way: "Behavior isn't goal directed it is goal interpreted" (p. 195). He means that a project is made more sensible once a history has been imported into it. We do not need to assume, says Weick, that people organize to accomplish, through orderly action, some previously agreed-on end. Sometimes group goals are simply reviews of previous actions. How frequently, we wonder, and why, does such planning-after-the-fact occur?

Although Weick's ideas fit many groups, are useful, and must not be ignored, members who act first and later decide why they did so were initially brought together for a given reason, and the entity itself exists for that specific cause. Because members are already part of the unit, they probably are aware of and accepting of the unit's aim. This initial purpose describes what members will expect to happen, not what they have learned will occur on the basis of past experience. They require ahead of time that the group have an objective before they will ever take part in it. Perhaps a good proportion of the groups

Weick describes as creating unitary purposes after members act are in the process of changing these purposes, modifying them, or creating new ones. Perhaps they are merely making them more measurable. Or they may be making a show of force, acting because they are impatient or insecure, or trying to short-circuit arguments about what the group's mission should be. Group action is often taken, no doubt, with no clear purpose in mind. Eventually, however, members want a clear objective, so the vague one is better defined or a new one is chosen.

Conditions That Influence the Choice of an Initial Group Purpose

Both the procedure members follow when choosing a group purpose and the purpose they finally select can be influenced by many circumstances. Three of these are the environment of the group, the influence of supernatural events, and properties of the group itself (especially its size). We briefly note their potential impact.

Environment of the Group

Pressures arising outside a group can influence the choices made by decision makers in that unit. Most common are requests of persons who depend on the organization for help (clients) or demands of individuals who have the right to set requirements for the unit (bosses). We have noted earlier that the scores obtained by rival groups affect the plans of members. The objectives of these rival bodies also have an impact on the ideas of local planners—we can do whatever they can, and better. If competing organizations place weight on shady purposes, aggressive behavior, or shoddy output, members will feel forced to consider similar unethical purposes for their own unit. What the surrounding community wants of an organization may also modify the group's purpose, as will the ways groups are used in a given culture. Companies in Sweden, Japan, and Nova Scotia, for example, are urged, more than in the United States or France, to pay as much attention to the needs of employees as to their desire for company profit (see Chapter Seven).

Influence of Supernatural Events

Throughout history, humans have used the help of supernatural beings to develop purposes for their groups. These
spirits originally were created by their sponsors so they could be
available to assist people in time of need. In *The Birth of the
Gods* (1960, p. 7), Guy Swanson discusses the conditions that
cause members to invent such spirits. He distinguishes between
two typical qualities of the supernatural, *mana* and *spirits*.
"Mana is a substance or essence that gives one the ability to perform tasks or achieve ends otherwise impossible. It increases
natural ability and confers supernatural skills." Mana may be
directed, for citizens on this earth, toward the achievement of
individual purposes, or those of a group or both. Through
magic or religious ceremonies, humans try to infuse mana with
their own purposes and thereby to change for the better how
mana affects them or their groups. A spirit is a supernatural
being that has personal purposes and complete power to achieve
those objectives. Moreover, a spirit (unlike a being in the natural world) needs only to want something and it will happen. If
rain is desired, water begins falling as soon as this idea comes to
mind. A spirit needs to make no effort and do no work (beyond
thinking) in order to bring a desire about and can make things
happen for people on Earth at whim. Humans therefore need to
make spirits want what they want in order to obtain heavenly
help.

Members of a worldly group develop special attributes for
their body that Swanson calls a *constitution*. This contains their
plans, procedures, policies, and purposes. Each group has an
area of sovereignty, a site where it has a legitimate right to perform in particular ways. Members realize that certain spirits
have their own preferences and therefore influence events that
concern their earthly group. Spirits may help or hinder things
done in behalf of that unit. Thus when matters do not go well
in the unit, or poor results are feared, members ask (pray) for
help from a particular spirit. The spirit will improve matters if
inclined to do so. Some spirits foster only certain groups and
not others. Each deity, moreover, suits the constitution of a
particular group—a godly division of labor. There are, as well,

special spirits having responsibility for a particular kind of group sovereignty. Clearly, such gods bear directly on the choice of a group's purpose; in some places, they are the major source of influence.

Properties of the Group

Once a group has established a particular purpose, members are not likely to accept objectives that oppose it or even think seriously of ones that are dissonant with it. Thus a collective created to help members learn how to relax is not likely to conduct a campaign for a political candidate. Standards created to govern policies, procedures, personnel, or ethics in a group will favor some kinds of purposes but exclude others. The size of an organization and the arrangements among its people, departments, or buildings make certain purposes logical and others impossible. The amount of energy members invest in maintaining their organization also affects the acceptability of certain group goals. Such influences originating in the group's environment and in the qualities of the group itself need to be studied more closely. The method of coping with stress preferred by an organization's top officers can permeate the way of life among members of an organization. Kets de Vries and Miller (1984) report that the neurotic characteristics of top executives are reflected in their firms. The authors describe five kinds of companies: dramatic, depressive, paranoid, compulsive, and schizoid. Each type is generated by officials with that particular "diagnosis."

Let us examine the effects of a group's size on its purposes and programs. We noted earlier that national associations are more often interested in serving their members (reflexive purposes) than in influencing nonmembers (transitive purposes). But this contrast (reflexive versus transitive) is probably not an effect of large size alone because many large organizations that are not associations (corporations, chain stores, government agencies, military units) are devoted exclusively to having an impact on persons outside the group.

Large and small organizations differ, we anticipate, in certain properties of their purposes. Because bigger units are ordinarily more imposing than smaller bodies, their purposes can be more powerful and important than those of the lesser units. But sheer bigness makes most operations more unwieldy in a social body. Thus the purposes of large organizations may be harder to achieve (they are less accessible), more resistant to change (less flexible), and more incompatible (less consonant one with another). There is no obvious reason, however, that large and little groups naturally differ in the measurability, co-operativeness, or difficulty of the group's purposes.

In huge organizations (religious sects, professional societies, political parties, or fraternal societies), it will be difficult to select or change purposes if members have a right to participate in this decision. Yet some massive units do change their direction easily because a handful of officers are authorized to make this change for the entire body without asking members to approve the modification. Within a large institution, there can be a number of departments, and each of these develop purposes for themselves and the parent body. When this is the case, a big organization may be torn more strongly than a small one by intergroup conflicts over its aims and motives.

In a big organization, a larger proportion of members are less likely to know the purposes of the agency, understand them, or be guided by them because information about these matters may not reach the rank and file. Ordinary members are concerned with their daily duties and leave it to their superiors to know what the body is trying to accomplish. It is harder, therefore, to keep a group purpose alive and useful in a larger organization.

Finally, implementing the purposes of a large organization is more complicated than doing so in a small unit. There are more activities to be performed in separated parts of the body, and these must be coordinated in ways that suit the greater goal of all parts. Doubtless, a bigger unit has more inappropriate activities therefore than a smaller one does.

Summary

Individuals who develop a group or become members of it want that unit to have a purpose for its activities. They have this requirement for several reasons. The purpose provides a direction for activities, and members are uncomfortable if they do not have this guide. It tells members what they ought to do and what they can expect of colleagues. It offers a criterion for evaluating whether the efforts of members are as effective as they ought to be. It is a focus for the personal commitment a member might make to that unit. It may serve, after the fact, as a rationalization for actions members take before they have a precise aim for their efforts. It reduces participants' sense of aimlessness in their work for that unit.

A group has a purpose because it is assigned to the whole or chosen by members. As the body becomes a stronger unit, members' wish for a group purpose also increases.

Although obscure purposes give vague guidance to members, many organizations live with them well. One reason is that each member can serve personal goals when the group's goal is imprecise and can assume that private plans are covered and made proper by the group's general or loose aims. Vague ends are tolerated by inventing, alongside them, measurable and accessible goals that serve to guide and evaluate actions for members. These may have some or little relevance to the initial, more general objectives.

Persons responsible for deciding on a group's purpose may improve on their decision making by more freely using their intuition and imagination. They can become more creative by finding out what comparable groups are doing, setting a deadline for persons charged with defining objectives, seeking purposes that best fit an ideal, or by ignoring disharmony among chosen objectives.

The basis for a group's purpose can be established by defining the identity of the organization. The identity is found in answers to two questions: What is this group? What should it become?

Additional Readings

Ansoff, H. I. *Corporate Strategy*. New York: McGraw-Hill, 1965. Describes the use of objective data in planning for the future of a firm.

Christopher, W. *The Achieving Enterprise.* New York: American Management Association, 1974. Provides practical advice on how to determine the identity and programs of an organization.

Cohen, M., and March, J. *Leadership and Ambiguity.* New York: McGraw-Hill, 1974. Problems caused for a president of a university by the obscurity of the school's purposes.

Cyert, R. M., and March, J. G. *A Behavioral Theory of the Firm.* Englewood Cliffs, N.J.: Prentice-Hall, 1963. An explanation of the methods officials use for selecting goals and procedures in a company.

Delbeca, A. L., Van de Ven, A. H., and Gustafson, D. H. *Group Techniques for Program Planning.* New York: Scott, Foresman, 1975. Describes the nominal group technique and the Delphi process for making decisions in groups.

Janis, I., and Mann, L. *Decision Making.* New York: Free Press, 1977. An analysis of the steps a person or group takes in making decisions that are important to the deciders.

SIX

Effects
of Individual
and Group Values

In Texas, a crew of retired men move throughout the state building small churches without charging for their work. If a congregation can buy needed lumber and land but not labor, this company will erect a house of worship the hosts could not otherwise afford. The builders accept no payment, they explain, because they love the Lord and want to help neighbors who believe as they do. They work for good, not for gain. Clearly, their values do not resemble those of most building contractors.

Nature of Group Values

How values modify members' choice of a group purpose is not well understood because this question has not been studied. We can develop a bit of insight into the matter by recalling how values usually guide people's regular beliefs and actions. A value is concerned with appropriate beliefs, not with ends to be achieved. A *value*, for a group member, is that individual's concept of an ideal kind of behavior. The member uses this notion to assess the goodness or badness, the rightness or wrongness, of actions by participants in the unit. A value describes things that should be done or should be avoided without fail, not merely behavior that is attractive or disliked. It delineates moral efforts from immoral ones and is an absolute good under all circumstances. Persons develop some values for themselves, but more often they are taught what ones to follow or obey. Once they commit themselves to a given value, there is no excuse for not adhering to it always.

Some values constrain individuals who are acting on their own. Examples are be honest, be courageous, be energetic, be self-sufficient, be unemotional. Other values guide interaction among individuals: for example, take turns, help one another, compete vigorously against a rival, winning is everything. Or values may delimit a group to be productive, nurturant, conservative, courageous, or faithful. A value that is rigid and without adequate grounds is called a *dogma*.

Milton Rokeach (1973, 1979) conceives of values as enduring, transcendental beliefs that guide one's conduct and serve as standards of behavior. Rokeach makes a distinction between what he calls *terminal* values, which are guides for a lifetime, and *instrumental* values, which are modes of conduct appropriate at this place and hour. Examples of terminal values are loving, helping, and telling the truth. Organizations are frequently created because their developers prize, and wish to foster, terminal states, such as freedom, fairness, or reverence. Groups are also formed to implement instrumental values, such as caring or cooperating.

Throughout history, people have conceived of special values to help them reduce their uncertainty about the following sorts of issues: What kind of pleasure is proper? How hard should one work? How are differences in social status justified? When is honesty not the best policy? When is it better to compete (or cooperate) with colleagues? What are products of human efforts, compared to God's efforts? Why does God create pain and misfortune? Are humans born good or evil? What should a group expect of a member? Do humans control their own fate? Is one's course after death already ordained at birth? What property should be public, what private? People in groups, associations, nations, and religions differ in their answers to questions such as these. In Lebanon, there are ten different Christian sects whose members have fought and killed one another for centuries because of their contrasting beliefs about such issues.

Members typically support values that are important to their way of life in that organization. William Scott (1965) observed this when he studied the values of students in Greek-letter societies at a state university. He identified the following values as most salient to the members: intellectualism, kindness, social skill, loyalty, academic achievement, physical development, status, honesty, religiousness, self-control, creativity, and independence. The beliefs that caused most guilt to a member who transgressed them were religiousness, independence, self-control, and honesty. Those that generated least guilt if transgressed were loyalty, status, and creativity. The fraternities and sororities recruited members whose values were similar to those views already prized by veterans in the units. The societies did not change the values of new members through social pressures because persons they recruited already had the "correct" views.

Values advocated in a business firm are not entirely the same as those fostered in an association such as a fraternity or sorority. Peters and Waterman (1982) report that the views given weight in companies, especially in more successful firms, are beliefs in the importance of the following:

• Doing better than rival organizations
• Giving details all the attention they deserve
• Treating each person as an individual
• Providing a superior quality of product and service
• Encouraging innovativeness by members
• Creating the informality needed for easy communication among members
• Emphasizing economic growth and profits of the firm

Some of these guide the organization acting as a whole; others guide individuals while doing their jobs or interacting with colleagues. The values given most weight in a business enterprise may vary from country to country. As an example, Caves and Uekusa (1976, p. 7) speak of the ideas fostered in a Japanese company. "The pursuit of profit, like the activity of selling, has never been held in high esteem in Japan. Thus the business goals of some entrepreneurs and groups seem to be substitutes for the goal of pursuing profit. . . . Insuring the continuity and growth of the commercial house became an important rationalization for business activities' insuring the honor, probity, and growth of the house." Think, moreover, of how values in doing business may differ between Russians, Chinese, Nigerians, Lebanese, South Africans, and Swedes.

Whitely (1979) compared decisions made by more than seven hundred business managers in Australia and India. Some of these administrators (called *pragmatists*) were known, on the basis of previous testing, to put practical matters first; others (called *moralists*) put proper behavior first. Regardless of their value-orientation, the strength of these views, or their nationality, the decisions of the managers, either for their personal good or for the group they supervised, were strongly influenced by the values they held. That is, pragmatists gave practical considerations more weight than moral ones, and moralists placed moral matters ahead of practical issues. Whitely based his research on a theory proposed by England (1976) that describes how values limit the behavior and perceptions of managers in different cultures, regardless of contrasts among the values involved.

Some values are more potent than others. Professional athletes, for example, make their own ethical codes and hire officials to enforce these regulations. Each set of rules is based on beliefs about good sportsmanship and fairness of rewards from competition. Such rules seem to be followed closely among golfers, speedboat racers, and archers but are often evaded by track-runners and tennis players. Or perhaps it is a matter of how well their rules are enforced. Among scientists prior to 1950, one seldom heard of a researcher faking results to be able to report better findings than those actually obtained. In recent years, however, when funds for research are more available to workers who publish more technical articles, it is not uncommon to learn of researchers who reported events they never actually observed. The scholars' desire to make a significant contribution and to win more grants leads them to ignore values of scientific ethics.

Lately, as we already noted, there has been an increase in the number of organizations devoted to reducing pollution and preserving natural lands. Douglas and Wildavsky (1982) remark that these bodies are actively committed to values of human goodness, equality of status, purity of heart, and purity of mind. As members of these associations see it, a worldliness and a conspiracy in big organizations leads them to oppose the values of the environmentalists and to favor instead big money and selfish values of the marketplace. Members expect to find collaboration and collusion among local spoilers of the environment. They believe they can best expose these plots through the work of small-scale subunits, each with less than a dozen members, rather than one large body. These antipollution squads refuse to compromise on any issue and tend to favor intolerance, drastic solutions, minimal organizational structure, and few rules. They guard against infiltration of their group by unsympathetic outsiders and seek purity in all their activities, not only in environmental matters. They underscore their singular opinions by demonstrating their uniqueness in other ways, such as their dress, food, craftsmanship, and admiration of the simple life. Their objectives are global in range, although their actions are community centered. They prize moral fervor and seek to arouse righteous enthusiasm in others.

The objectives of a unit may foster new values or remind members that special values are significant to the group, especially those values that caused the purpose to be worded as it is. A team of mountain climbers, for instance, learns to place special emphasis on safety and mutual protection among teammates. A company trying to survive a sudden financial loss stresses the importance of reducing waste and costs. Furthermore, a value can provide a justification for actions members ordinarily would avoid or it may be invented to give meaning to members' behavior. Personal immobility, for example, may become wise, rather than a sign of laziness, when the weather is too hot to exert oneself. In India, as a case in point, passiveness became a virtue (a time of meditation) because it is not pleasant to work hard in that steamy climate. Also, one may be abjectly obedient and readily accept pressures to conform if one has little power to disobey and dares not transgress rules established by powerful others. The code of behavior composed by Confucius was originally a justification for demands made by distant and impersonal officials of ancient China. Peasants adhered to the code and came to see it as delineating the correct way to live. Many of the norms laid down by Confucius still guide behavior in Oriental countries. The Buddhas, each of whom founded a different sect, originally were wise men who made suggestions for proper demeanor and views toward life. These sages did not expect their ideas to become the basis for a religion.

Effects of Group Values

Because values differ from place to place and from group to group, it seems likely that the purposes chosen in these sites and bodies will also differ. Consider, as an example, students of group behavior over the world. These scholars differ, from country to country, in the content of their research concerning relations between a member and a group. In the United States, a scientist emphasizes how a group restricts a member's freedom and creates unfavorable consequences for the individual's personal life. In Russia, how a group fosters growth in a member's character is studied; in France, how a person exerts pressure to change colleagues or superiors; in Japan, how a member helps the group to perform at its best. These dissimilar research topics reflect differences among scholars' value-laden beliefs.

In early Greece, discussing philosophy, reading poetry, or arguing about social issues was as popular among ordinary citizens as watching athletic contests is today. The Olympic games devoted as much time to debates and speaking contests as they did to athletic competition because Greeks put high value on group discussion, rational thinking, and careful use of words. All questions were open for perusal, and answers were replaced with better ones if these later came to hand. In Italy, as a contrast, Christianity created criteria for correct behavior, and founders of that religion established procedures for ensuring that members conformed to fixed beliefs. Doubt was forbidden. Those who did not believe were tortured, banished, and denied rewards that the church alone could provide. Thus creeds and unquestioning faith were important in Italy, and logic, innovation, and the solving of problems were important in Greece.

The values of political parties are as potent in the modern world as religious beliefs have been in other days. Contrasting opinions between parties with such names as Christian Democrats, Fascists, Nazis, Peronistas, Conservatives, Laborites, Republicans, and Communists are based on dissimilar conceptions about man, learning, economics, welfare, free will, decision making, religion, social power, and property. Fundamental opinions change, however, as circumstances make such a shift necessary and as each generation establishes its own way of life by shedding ideas from the past. When a political party becomes dominant in a country, it presses citizens to adopt its values. In China under Mao, this was done thoroughly by requiring every citizen to spend hours meeting with neighbors in small discussion groups each week for months and years. There they learned to lead their lives in ways approved by the new officials of their nation (Whyte, 1974).

Some writers assume and deplore that the values of organizations are given more weight in society than the values of individuals. According to this view, each manager and member does only what is necessary to help the association as a whole but not the individuals who are members. There is no personal right or wrong, only what is good for the group. Whatever is best for an individual, moreover, can only come from an organization (Whyte, 1956; Scott and Hart, 1979). Such writers believe, in short, that individual values should always take precedence over group-based ones. No doubt they often do.

Units with different values generate different styles of behavior. Consider how dissimilarly each of the following four groups (listed here according to their values) would probably behave because their members believe in one set of values more than another: (1) love, happiness, peace, freedom; (2) profit, productivity, efficiency, growth; (3) faith, reverence, self-control, loyalty; (4) team spirit, perseverance, active pursuit, anger, aggressiveness. Recently I saw two groups of musicians, a week apart, on the same platform. The first group, a double quartet of singers, marched on the stage. They were erect, in a single file, smiling, and dressed in well-cut tuxedos. They showed alert energy, looked into the eyes of observers and appeared to enjoy entertaining. They sang tightly arranged melodies in which close harmony was required among them. They preferred precise tones and an exact blending of these. No one was a solo star. Watchers applauded the group as a whole. The second group, a jazz band, came on the stage slowly, one at a time, in rumpled and informal clothing. They leaned about, chatting and ignoring the audience, looking bored and tired. When the leader arrived (late) and they began to play, each member took a turn showing his skill while the rest of the orchestra made background sounds. This group placed value on the spontaneous creativity of its separate individuals and on their variations on a melodic theme. The audience applauded each member individually, in turn, for his solo performance.

If values of members, or of those in a group's environment, influence decisions about a group's purpose, we expect stronger beliefs to have a stronger impact. The *strength* of a value is the amount of influence it has on the choice of a group's objectives and on the activities of members. Tools exist to help in studying such matters. There are, for instance, paper-and-pencil questionnaires for measuring which values among a specified set are most important to respondents. These tests were developed by Rokeach (1973, 1979) and by Scott (1965). Newcomb (1961) used the Allport-Vernon (1951) measure of values in his research on the development of friendships among students who lived in the same rooming house. We need ways of identifying which values, among all kinds conceivable, have most weight in specific groups.

In a group with centralized leadership, it is common for executives to designate the values that are to be most important in that agency and to make sure that these guide the behavior of members. Managers make values visible by speaking and writing about them. They stress the significance of their favorite ones by acting in accord with them, praising colleagues who do likewise, and disapproving of co-workers who deviate from these standards. Managers, as a consequence, probably prefer group purposes that suit their own personal values. They tend, moreover, to press subordinates toward values that superiors think are important (Peters and Waterman, 1982).

Because a group-supported value delineates what a member should or should not do, each belonger tries to abide by its limits and expects others to conform to these as well. A member, accordingly, puts pressures on others to behave as is expected in that unit. This pressure is made more potent if all participants in an organization discuss which values are precious to them and then agree as a body to abide by the decision they reach. After such an agreement, expectations guided by values are taken to be more legitimate and therefore more acceptable to all. Interpersonal power among members increases, moreover, as the group becomes more *cohesive*: that is, as members have a stronger wish to remain as members (Cartwright and Zander, 1968). Persons who are more strongly attracted to membership are more willing to do what others ask so that they can be approved by colleagues and retained as members. Also, persons who are more attracted to a group will exert stronger pressures on associates in order to help the group be effective and survive. The power of a group to influence the values of its members, in short, is a function of the cohesiveness of that group.

A value with greater weight among members inspires them to prevent behavior that does not suit that value. Some organizations employ confessional conferences, group counseling, subterfuge, or spies to discover covert transgression of values by members. If wrong thoughts or behaviors are uncovered, members try to rehabilitate the deviant provided that this person is useful enough to warrant the effort or the value is important enough to justify those measures. In Japan, unlike most countries, a person who has been a miscreant, wishes to reform, and is not able to make the change alone can get help in changing beliefs. To modify their thinking, such individuals are required by a counselor to sit in the corner of a room, on the floor, behind a screen, for a week or so. These "reformees" spend their time thinking about the harm that their bad behavior or thoughts have caused those closest to them at home, in the community, and in the workplace. The counselor joins the client once or twice a day to help the latter feel guilty about incorrect thoughts or behavior. As a result, the person in the corner develops an overwhelming sense of regret, a new appreciation of the values transgressed, and an increased realization that relevant values are important to colleagues as well. An account of this method for changing values is provided by Lebra (1976).

Some values inspire behavior among members that causes a whole unit to be viewed unfavorably by those in its environment. The members of an organization are likely to be disapproved if they demand unwelcome changes in society, attack nonmembers, or act in ways that are unethical or sacrilegious. Some popular values generate side effects that were not foreseen when they were made a part of the group's code. An emphasis on harmony among members, for instance, may create comfort in interpersonal relations at the cost of preventing differences in opinion, creative conflicts, or effective problem solving (Janis, 1972). Openness in communication may lead to unfair evaluations of one another or to undue pressure between individuals. Urging greater productivity by a group as a whole can lead members to indulge in shortcuts that damage the quality of its output.

Summary

A member's most precious belief, called a value, is the concept of an ideal kind of behavior within that unit. The individual uses this concept to assess the goodness or badness, the rightness or wrongness of actions by participants. Values differ from group to group because assemblages of members differ and because contrasting environments foster dissimilar values from time to time and from culture to culture. Organizations harboring unlike values differ, then, in their activities. A stronger group value places firmer constraints on the choice of a group's purpose.

Additional Readings

Douglas, M., and Wildavsky, A. *Risk and Culture.* Berkeley: University of California Press, 1982. A description of groups engaged in citizens' actions to improve the environment and control toxic wastes.

Peters, T. J., and Waterman, R. H. *In Search of Excellence.* New York: Harper & Row, 1982. Describes how successful firms set and support strong values.

Rokeach, M. *The Nature of Human Values: Individual and Societal.* New York: Free Press, 1973. The importance of values in the lives of people and how to measure them.

Scott, W. *Values and Organizations.* Skokie, Ill.: Rand McNally, 1965. The effect of members' values on their behavior in groups.

Zander, A. "The Value of Belonging to a Group in Japan." *Small Group Behavior,* 1983, *14,* 3-14. A discussion of the basic premises behind the role of groups in Japan and the United States.

SEVEN

How Individual
and Group Motives
Influence Group Purposes

When individuals select a purpose for a group they not only seek to modify certain conditions (as we saw in Chapters Two and Three) but also want to satisfy desires aroused in that situation. They may have had these dispositions for some time or developed them while considering the need for a group and a purpose. Whether long-standing or newly learned, their wishes affect the nature of the objectives they prefer for their unit. Such hopes may be due to *self-oriented motives* for pride, fun, help, purity, excitement, knowledge, or the solution of a problem. Or their choice of a purpose may be influenced by a *group-oriented desire* for the unit as a whole concerning its success, harmony, productivity, influence, or nurturance.

Motives and Incentives: Some Definitions

A *motive*, whether self- or group-oriented, is a capacity to find satisfaction in the attainment of a specific incentive and a disposition to seek that satisfaction. Motives develop because individuals' experiences teach them to have certain wants. Some motives are the result of private and personal plans; others are the product of interpersonal pressures among members. Maslow (1954) proposes that particular motives are not arousable until others with higher priority are first cared for. In his view, individuals must settle types of needs in this order:

1. Physiological demands
2. Personal safety
3. Belongingness
4. Esteem
5. Self-actualization

Among a given collection of people, individuals probably form groups to deal with needs that appear later in this list only after they have satisfied ones at an earlier level. Self-actualizing bodies (groups to help people develop their talents) will not be developed, for example, unless members have few unsettled physiological problems (such as hunger, health, rest), are secure, feel they belong, and are not suffering from a sense of inferiority. Such a hypothesis merits investigation.

An *incentive* is a state or outcome that, when attained, provides satisfaction for a person with a given motive. The presence of an incentive also serves to arouse the relevant motive. Typical incentives are a score, financial gain, friendship, food, fun, and approval by colleagues. Carron (1980) reports that young people believe a number of incentives can be satisfied through participation in team sports. These include high status among friends, excellence in the sport, intimidating opponents, excitement in contests, making new friends, and doing things on one's own. An individual who has a self-oriented motive to succeed has a proclivity to be satisfied upon achieving success. If the motive is to influence particular persons, satisfaction will be derived from inducing changes in their behavior. Some persons have many motives; others have few. Some want to fulfill a given motive (if it is aroused) and work hard to do so; others do not care much about that special need. Incentives vary in their *incentive value*: that is, they differ in the amount of satisfaction they promise to provide a person. The amount of incentive value one anticipates in an upcoming event is the result of one's past reaction to situations similar to it or to the reaction of other persons. The amount of value assigned to a given incentive can be changed. This is why parents, teachers, character builders, and psychotherapists try to increase the incentiveness of desirable situations and to reduce the value of less appropriate ones: the intent is to modify an individual's sources of satisfaction and change in turn the individual's behavior. A group's purpose or goal, as we shall see, is simply a special kind of incentive.

The *perceived probability of an incentive* is the likelihood, as an individual sees things, that the condition that generates satisfaction is achievable. People may have strong motives and place strong value on pertinent incentives, but these views will not affect their behavior if they believe they cannot attain the state that would furnish satisfaction for them.

Self-oriented motives dispose members to seek personal gains, thus decisions about life in a group may be so made that the unit will satisfy these motives. They often aim the body so members can help one another fulfill personal hopes all share alike. For instance, persons who are similarly afraid to fly in an airplane, who like to sing, who love old gasoline engines, or who hate the boss equally well gather and create means for mutually meeting their related wishes. Usually, these group-planned methods are better than ones an individual can develop alone. The group's purpose recognizes both the legitimacy of members' similar but personal motives and that some individuals get more out of the group than others do. Members might agree to define and develop one specific, common, personal motive and foster joint attempts to satisfy that desire to, for example, lose weight, bolster self-regard, improve investments, or support sobriety. They may, in contrast, decide that the group will tolerate or encourage a variety of dissimilar individual motives among members, and the aim of the group will then be to help belongers satisfy these varied personal hopes. Schools, studios, and convalescent centers are units of this type.

In numerous groups, the main interest of members is in what happens to the group as an institution, or in what the group creates while acting as a unit. Colleagues may have a strong desire for their group to be influential. Perhaps they are parts of a citizens' committee for improved schools, and they choose a joint purpose that allows them to demonstrate their power in relations with the local board of education. This might be to get favorite candidates elected to the board or to influence members of the board by speaking at its meetings. They may write letters to the editors or pamphlets on education in that community to further these ends. Teams, business firms, or special commissions are likewise devoted to the good of the group more than they are to the gain of each member.

We are more interested here in members' motives for the group as a whole than in motives for personal benefit because group-oriented desires more readily stimulate participants to decide what the group is and what it may become. We recognize that individuals in an organization may have both personal and group-centered aspirations and that they may be driven by dual sets of motives to fulfill private yearnings for their own good and to help their organization succeed. Clearly, a group will go along better if members have appropriate uniformity in their points of view about where the group should be heading and why. More on this later.

Several unsolved theoretical problems arise when we assume that members can achieve a consensus concerning the group's end state. How shall members' separate objectives for their group be combined? Should we take an average? ask for a vote? require unanimity? How can we use the fact that some members have goals for themselves or the group that they do not mention aloud, even while they follow these secret plans? When several motives are aroused at once, which influences their behavior? The strongest? These issues deserve study (Ziman, 1978).

Values and Motives Compared

A motive encourages specific behavior. So does a value. How are they similar and how are they different? A motive can become so stringent that it operates like a value, while a value can become so arousing that it functions like a motive (Feather,

when it accomplishes a challenging task where its outcome is the responsibility of the unit as one body, not of some one member acting alone. The *perceived probability of group success* (*Pgs*) is the likelihood, as members see it, that their group can accomplish its chosen goal (that is, the subjective difficulty of the goal for the group). The *incentive value of group success* (*Igs*) is the amount of satisfaction members believe they will attain from the group's accomplishment of its task. The *tendency* to try for group success (*Tgs*) is a function of the desire to achieve group success (*Dgs*), the perceived probability of group success (*Pgs*), and the incentive value of group success (*Igs*). Thus, $Tgs = Dgs \times Pgs \times Igs$. A self-oriented motive and a group-oriented desire operate in a similar fashion.

In contrast, the tendency to avoid group failure (*Tagf*) is a joint function of three conditions: the *desire to avoid group failure* (*Dagf*), the *perceived probability of group failure* (*Pgf*), and the *incentive value of group failure* (*Igf*). The desire to avoid group failure is a disposition to experience embarrassment for or loss of pride in one's group following its failure. That is, $Tagf = Dagf \times Pgf \times Igf$.

Because the tendency to achieve group success (*Tgs*) may be stronger or weaker than the tendency to avoid group failure (*Tagf*), a resultant tendency to action by members is determined by whichever is stronger, *Tgs* or *Tagf*. Thus, the resultant tendency for group achievement is determined by $Tgs - Tagf$. Members accordingly work to attain the attractive consequences of success, to avoid the repulsive consequences of failure, or to do one more than the other. More generally, members work to achieve satisfaction in the group, to avoid dissatisfaction, or to do one more than the other. These contrasting desires, as we shall see, call forth different kinds of purposes from members.

Results of research on the effects of the desire for group achievement (*Dgs*) show what members of a group can do to increase a unit's chances of success (Zander, 1971). These include choosing a challenging goal (not too easy or too hard), measuring amount of movement toward that goal, reporting the degree of this movement to members, changing the goal when necessary, improving skills where necessary, practicing methods for performing the group's work, improving procedures used in the group's task, keeping tools reliable, arousing members' desire for group success, raising confidence in their chances of success, recruiting talented persons, or acquiring more resources (see Chapter Eight).

What do members do when they have a strong tendency to avoid failure by the group? An obvious defense against failure is to do whatever is needed for a success or to avoid that activity. But, when members are constrained to work on the group's task and are dominated by a tendency to avoid the consequences of failure because they have often failed and therefore fear they will fail again, they do not always work for a success and the pride it provides. Instead, they seek to evade the embarrassment a group's failure generates because they recognize that, given their group's past record of failures, the chances of being successful are poor. The methods members of such a group choose to use in working toward that end make it probable that a success will be precluded for them. These methods are choosing an impossibly difficult goal so that members need not be ashamed of failure (but can be proud of their high ambition), misrecalling the group's score so it appears to be better than it actually was, denying that members were at fault, asserting that they have done well enough for most purposes, getting rid of all group goals so these cannot be used as criteria for success, claiming they are not embarrassed by the group's performance, or blaming faulty equipment, resources, or tools. In sum, members' anticipation of future group failure (because of past poor productivity) generates behavior that is conducive to further failure (Zander, 1971).

One further characteristic of achievement-oriented behavior is worthy of note. When members work on a group project but have no reliable evidence about how well their unit is doing (which is a frequent occurrence in standing committees and long-range missions), they tend to assume that their group is performing well and that the chances of its continuing to do so in the future are good. No news is good news. Apparently, this form of wishful thinking happens because members cannot accurately judge the probability of their group's success or failure. Their desire to succeed leads them to believe that the group actually is succeeding and will carry on in that fashion during days to come (Zander, 1971).

Members may also develop desires for their group that are not concerned with whether it does well on a particular task of more or less difficulty. Take the desire for a group to generate fun. This is the prime purpose of the Du Nothin Club, a weekly gathering of macho males who meet to eat, tell jokes, and kid one another. Despite its informal style, the group has officers, dues, a regular meeting place, and requirements for membership. The tendency of persons to take part in this tableside sport is the result of a desire for fun in the group (the incentive value of doing so) and the subjective probability that their togetherness will create the outcome they seek. It is plain that the skill of members in joking, their ability to stay within the bounds of good taste, and their need to avoid jocular hostility determine how well the luncheons in fact generate a sense of fun rather than pain. Any who are hurt by the give and take develop a desire to avoid that harm, a perceived probability of the chances that they will be hurt, and a dislike of being made uncomfortable. Their unfavorable views of the group will counter the group's initial intention and lower their inclination to show up for the luncheons. The purpose will be met only if the unit's jollity exceeds its cruelty.

Where does the desire for fun in a group come from? We can only guess what might generate this disposition. First, in the case of our club, it helps if members enjoy repartee and are skilled at it. But that is not enough. These men (or some of them) must also be together on some occasion and recognize that they are having fun as a group, more than they would if each were alone. They must like the kind of spirit that develops among them and must believe that members are willing to assemble and to form a plan for activities that will lead to this condition at their meetings. They must realize that their banter can create hurt or disapproval and be able to limit such harm. They must believe that their desire for interpersonal fun is an adequate purpose for a group and that no more measurable, accessible, or noble ends are necessary in this case. In sum, members' desire for fun in the group arises from their pleasant experiences in interaction and from their effort to create conditions that help this style of relationship continue. Conceivably, this set of men could turn to a different procedure for fostering a different kind of fun (such as excursions, vaudeville shows, or tutoring youngsters in school). The same purpose would then be served by a different method.

In a contrasting vein, members may wish their group to have enough power to change the view of persons in the environment. When a decision of a group, or a statement released by the unit, changes how observers think, that body is said to have power over these persons. This influence is attributed to the entity as a whole, not to singular efforts of a few individuals in that body. Some groups try to influence particular persons in particular ways. Members of a labor union want their activities to affect what managers do, and therefore officers of the union get the help of the local's brothers and sisters in making their group powerful. A typical method for doing this is to hold a strike. Leaders urge members to join the picket line, making it clear to them that by doing so they can win the minds of managers, that this is a sensible thing to do, and that the work stoppage will probably have the desired effect. Workers' enthusiasm for patrolling the picket line will not be aroused, however, if they feel that the strike will weaken their power to persuade the managers rather than increase it and that they had better avoid the stoppage or turn to other sources of power for their union.

How do members develop a desire for their group to be influential? Most commonly, this occurs when individuals recognize that each, acting alone, is deprived in some respect and that they can overcome this deprivation through joining in a group with others who also want a change. Members may feel disadvantaged because of actions by someone who has power to control their fate. As a consequence, the members seek to develop skills, resources, or allies that will increase their group's power. Or persons may join a group that already has influence and then help defend and improve that capacity and its aims. All in all, members want their group to have power when such power will help the group create or maintain conditions that members desire.

Origin of Members' Desire for Group Success

Returning to a group at work, let us assume that a unit's task is one it must repeat periodically (making objects, planning a new approach for each year, running an annual financial campaign, or administering a hospital day by day) and that, on the completion of each trial or several time periods, the group has a quantitative result, such as dollars received, products made, patients cured, or waste created. Members may recognize that some scores are easy to reach and others are difficult but may not yet know what score their group is able to earn consistently, what its best achievement might be, what other units can do on this kind of activity, or what would be an easy (or unfeasible) action for this group. They realize that, in the abstract, getting a high score is more satisfying than getting a low one and that the array of all possible scores, from easy to hard, provides a scale of excellence. A higher level is closer to excellence than a lower one, but a higher score is also harder to accomplish than an easier one. What should they aspire to do?

After experience in its activity, members can better estimate what their unit will accomplish, given its personnel, resources, training, experience, procedures, and the like. This seasoning also helps them assess what level of accomplishment is too hard for the group and what is too easy for it. Generally speaking, members believe that, although their group will not attain a *very* high score, the score it does reach will probably be higher rather than lower on the scale of excellence. They assign a *perceived probability of group success (Pgs)* for each available score during a number of trials. On the basis of their work in that activity, members also hunch about the chances of failure by their group. A member's *perceived probability of group failure (Pgf)* is that individual's judgment of the probability that the group will fail to attain each potential score. Such predictions can be made for each conceivable level of aspiration. Judgment will be based on the assumption that the group is less certain to fail on an easy score than on a difficult one. Note that the probability of future success *(Pgs)* is the inverse of the probability of future failure *(Pgf)*; thus perceived probability of success increases as perceived probability of failure decreases, and the sum of the two probabilities equals zero.

When subjective estimates about a group's potential are in hand, members react to later evidence about the unit's attainment in a way that is no longer simply cognitive. Their anticipation about the group's future scores now generates affect-laden responses to the group's output: members are pleased if the group does better than it had been expected to do and are disappointed if it does not do as well. An improved score means to members that the group is moving closer to excellence, a worse score that the group is losing its skill. Members' reaction to succeeding is a forerunner of the incentive value of group success. A favorable response is stronger for a better score and weaker for a poorer one. The *incentive value of group success* (Igs), then, is the amount of satisfaction in the group that a member develops following attainment of a given level of achievement. In contrast, the *incentive value of group failure* (Igf) is the amount of dissatisfaction in the group that a member develops following its failure to reach a given target. Thereafter, any score by the group serves members as a source of more or less satisfaction or more or less dissatisfaction. Participants now have developed a desire for group achievement. Often, this desire is the result of an overt groupwide vote among all members and thus is a visible property of the whole unit.

A member's satisfaction with the group's performance is greater if it has completed a difficult level than if it has finished an easier one. Also, a member's dissatisfaction is less after a failure to finish a harder job than after a failure to accomplish an easier one. Thus dissatisfaction over a group's failure to attain a given score (Igf) is inversely related to the perceived probability of failure (Pgf) to attain that level.

When members hope their group will gain a certain score and plan to compare the group's later output with that expectation, they have in mind a goal for their group—a state they want the group to accomplish. Note that they can set this goal rationally only if they have reliable evidence about their group's actual scores. What other considerations influence their choice of a goal for their group?

Motives for Choosing a Group's Goal

Ordinarily, members prefer a goal that will provide as much satisfaction as is reasonably possible. Difficult ones may be perceived as not likely to yield satisfaction because they are too hard to reach. Easy ones may be seen as probably not satisfying because they provide weak self-approval when achieved. As persons choose a goal for their group, they consider both the amount of satisfaction derived from attaining that score and the probability of getting it. They also consider the amount of embarrassment a failure can bring to them. An unpleasant reaction to failure is greater if they miss on an easy task than if they fail on a hard one. The goal members favor for their group is placed, then, at the level of accomplishment that assures them the greatest probability of success (Pgs) and the greatest satisfaction from success (Igs) minus the level that assures the least probability of failure (Pgf) and the least dissatisfaction from failure (Igf). In short, a preferred goal is put at a level that is the resultant of $(Pgs \times Igs) - (Pgf \times Igf)$. Conditions in a group usually make one of these factors (on either side of the minus sign) stronger than the other (Zander, 1971). Thus, in their actions for the group, members emphasize either the desire for success or the desire to avoid failure.

We say that a group has a success when it reaches or exceeds a goal members have set for it. A group's success strengthens members' expectancy of future success: Pgs becomes stronger for more difficult levels, and members anticipate that the group will, in fact, perform better on levels that require more excellence. Also, a group's failure strengthens the expectancy of future failure: Pgf becomes larger as the group fails to do any better than reach easy levels. Because of the inverse relationship between incentive and probability, a group's success increases the desirability of success for members, and its failure increases the repulsiveness of failure. Thus the more difficult the goal is seen to be, the greater the perceived potential attractiveness of success and the less the potential repulsiveness of failure. Also, the easier the goal, the less the perceived potential attractiveness of success and the greater the potential repulsiveness of failure. A success heightens the attractiveness of future success, and a failure increases the repulsiveness of future failure.

In a group activity that members repeat periodically while setting a new goal for each trial, the placement of a new target is influenced by members' evaluation of the group's prior performances: Did it do as well as members expected? By how much? As we will observe later (Chapter Eight), when a unit succeeds in attaining its goal, members tend to raise its goal for the next trial; and when the group fails, they tend to lower its goal. The rule is succeed, raise; fail, lower. It is noteworthy that they raise the goal more consistently after a success than they lower it after a failure and that they raise it by a greater amount after a success than they lower it after a failure. As a result, over a series of trials, the average level of a group's goal is above the average of the group's output. Thus, in the long run, groups fail more often than they succeed (Zander, 1971).

In a contrasting situation where the unit's work is one long, unending trial (as when members are writing a report, solving a special problem, or building a large structure), feedback about the group's progress often is unreliable because quantified scores are not available. When feedback is not available or is not trustworthy, we noted earlier, members tend to believe that the performance of their group is good. They thus set optimistic goals as though they were, in fact, succeeding. On a group activity that continues without repetition, members are most likely to feel their group is succeeding because they receive few reliable data about its progress.

When members have a stronger desire for group success (Dgs), research has shown that they prefer goals that are intermediate in difficulty—not too hard or too easy (Zander, 1971). To understand this preference for goals in the intermediate range of difficulty, let us suppose that the strength of $Dgs = 1$, that $Pgs = .90$ (an easy level), and that $Igs = .10$ (a success on that level is not very attractive). The product (Tgs) of these values is .09. Suppose next that Dgs again = 1, that $Pgs = .10$ (a much more difficult level), and that $Igs = .90$ (success on that level is very satisfying). The product (Tgs) of these values is again .09. Thus the tendency (Tgs) to move toward either a very hard or very easy goal is alike and weak. Suppose, now, that Dgs is still 1, that Pgs = .50 (an intermediate level of difficulty, halfway between .01 and 1.00), and Igs = .50 (success is moderately attractive). In this case, Tgs = .50 × .50 = .25, which is larger than the product .09 given earlier for either the hard or easy goal. Thus an intermediately difficult goal tends to create stronger Tgs than do harder or easier ones.

What happens as members' desire for group success increases in strength? If Dgs = 3, for instance, the easy score would have a Tgs of 3 × .09 = .27. The difficult score would also have a Tgs of .27, and the intermediate score a Tgs of 3 × .25 = .75. If Dgs were 5, these amounts would increase accordingly to .45, .45, and 1.25. Thus as Dgs increases, members become more interested in all goals, but especially in goals at the intermediate range of difficulty. When choosing a group goal, therefore, responsible members will more often choose one of intermediate difficulty as their desire for group success increases. This hypothesis has been supported in a variety of investigations (Zander, 1971). Indeed, members' tendency to choose goals of intermediate difficulty is a reasonably good indicator of the strength of Dgs among members.

Any situation that arouses participants' interest in doing well also stimulates anxiety over the prospects of doing poorly. As we noted a while ago, a tendency to avoid failure by the group ($Tagf$) is a resultant of the desire to avoid failure ($Dagf$), times the likelihood the group will fail (Pgf), times the unattractiveness of the consequences of failure (Igf). If $Tagf$ were stronger than Tgs and if members had a free choice to do what they wished as a group, members would prefer not to engage in the task at all and would avoid it. If, however, members are required to engage in the activity, perhaps by a person with great power, the resistance against doing so (due to the tendency to avoid failure) is stronger for the scores when the probability of failure is .50 (that is, an intermediate level) because this is the value where the expected negative value of failure is greatest. They will avoid goals of intermediate difficulty in favor of either very easy or very hard ones. They will think well of easy goals because the chances of failing are low (but the embarrassment is great if the group does fail on the easy task), and they will like hard goals because the embarrassment is little if they fail (even though the chances of failure to reach the goal are great). Groups with a history of failure tend to choose hard goals more than easy ones because they experience little chagrin when they do not attain a difficult score. Avoiding embarrassment, as we just noted, is more important to them than avoiding failure by working for an easy goal (Zander, 1977).

Ways to Increase the Strength of Dgs. Conditions that increase the strength of *Dgs* ensure that members will desire to work for group pride more than to avoid group embarrassment. A manager may encourage members to seek pride in their group's performance by acting in the following ways (Zander, 1982):

1. Emphasizing the sources of pride in their group—what causes pride to develop among members and what consequences it has for the group.
2. Increasing members' desire for group success by arranging the unit's goals, procedures, work plans, and resources so they help the group earn a good score. An excellent performance does not dull members' taste for further success; it makes high-quality work more desirable.
3. Helping the organization set clear goals. Members are more able to develop a desire for group success as the group's goals are more clearly defined. They cannot feel successful if they are uncertain about whether they have reached their group's objective or how they can do so.
4. Ensuring that group goals are realistic challenges for the membership and not unreasonably hard or easy. Because goals are standards of excellence for group activities, these should not be conducive to failure.
5. Making sure that all members understand what their individual contributions are to be to the final product of the group as a whole and that their work is valued by colleagues.
6. Privately indicating to members how membership in this

group is helpful to them as individuals so that each person will view the group as an attractive entity worthy of membership.

7. Making it clear to all that each teammate depends on the work of others if the group is to complete its task.

8. Emphasizing the unity of the group and its output as a team effort and that members in the group are serving its needs.

9. Being ready to change goals that are too difficult for the group. Satisfaction comes from living up to reasonable expectations, not from failing impossibly difficult ends.

10. Observing what obstacles prevent fulfillment of the group's goals and helping the group overcome these obstacles.

11. Encouraging talk in meetings about how performance can be improved and how the boring parts of the group's job can be made interesting.

12. Avoiding fear of failure and its subsequent tendency to evade challenges.

13. Helping members feel responsible for the group's fate. Members who know that the group's progress depends on their efforts want to provide good quality of work in their roles.

14. Giving members assignments that suit their abilities and provide them a feeling of competence. Members who think they are not competent develop the most concern about their personal failures and thus work to improve their personal output, not the group's.

The measurability or accessibility of a group's purpose has an impact on the probability that members can satisfy their desires for the group and therefore has an indirect effect on the strength of these desires. If the objective is obscure, those taking part in a group may be unable to obtain satisfaction of relevant motives because they do not know what steps to take in order to achieve the goal or how to measure their accomplishment. A vague purpose, therefore, seldom allows members to find full satisfaction. In contrast, if the purpose is measurable and accessible, members can see what and how much they must do to satisfy their desires. Typically, when members complete those things, their desire is satisfied. Participants lose interest in the old desire and move to other interests until the original one is again aroused. In sum, the vaguer a group's purpose, the longer members' desires that instigated this purpose may remain aroused, and the clearer the purpose, the sooner members lose interest in their initial desires for the group. Such thoughts lead us to the reasons for changes in the purposes of a group. These matters come up for consideration in Chapter Eight.

The desire among members to attain favorable group consequences and to avoid unfavorable ones modifies the kind of purpose decision makers select for a group. If members want the unit to be a place where interpersonal fun is facilitated, intergroup power wielded, abstinence encouraged, profit made, emotions aroused, or bodies repaired, they express this wish in one or more purposes for their group. Usually this kind of purpose is not a numerical quantity, such as a score or a dollar income, and is not a point along a scale of excellence, like the goals relevant to achieving success that we have just been considering. If the purpose is expressed in vague terms, it is not possible for members to know exactly what the incentive is and what the chances are that they can attain that satisfaction (because it is not measurable or accessible). Nevertheless, members usually find a way to make an assessment of whether they are fulfilling that purpose and, if not, to find a more agreeable target. Most members ignore obscure objectives, we believe, in favor of more precise aims. This assertion needs study to verify it, but consider the following.

Qualitative (Vague) Versus Quantitative (Clear) Goals. Broadly stated, a group's purpose can steer members' behavior more effectively if it is more measurable, more accessible, or both. If the purpose is clear (to cure patients, to provide a tool for research, to perform a symphony, or to foster participation in a group discussion), persons in the group know what to do toward that end and know when a desirable state of affairs has been sufficiently achieved.

But often, as we have seen, the purpose of a group is so

vague that members cannot know whether their unit is moving toward that aim or how to proceed in that direction. In such a case, they leave the initial purpose in place but give most of their attention to ends that are more accessible and measurable, cancel the initial purpose in favor of clearer objectives, or keep the original purpose and do not choose clearer states (even when they may work to attain simpler ends). Responsible members, we might guess, most often invent more measurable and accessible goals to supplement their group's vague purposes.

As a case in point, we examine a leisure-time group in which mutual acceptance of all comers, regardless of race, creed, or behavior, is a central aim. This might be a neighborhood potluck club, a group of foreign college students, a newcomers' association, or a self-help society. The founders hope to create a group where people of all kinds are comfortable. If the purpose of the group is for each to be accepted by all, how do participants tell if they are moving toward such a purpose?

The answer to this question is not obvious because there are pros and cons in efforts to create friendliness among people who ordinarily do not often mix. Members probably accept that it is good to have face-to-face contact with many persons in the group and that it is not proper to limit one's conversations to individuals with whom one feels most at ease. Even so, they discover that approaching strangers, especially those who are not like ones the approachers know best, can be embarrassing. It is easier to keep a distance from unfamiliar individuals. Thus the valued activity (approaching) is harder for them, and the less valued activity (avoiding) is easier. Because members are pressed to interact with all within the group, they eventually realize that practice in meeting new people makes interaction with the strangers less uncomfortable, and their awkwardness in associating with the aliens decreases a bit. A certain proportion of members become able to talk easily with one another. There is a limit, however, to the amount of time available for members to do more than chat briefly. Practice makes perfect, then, but slowly.

Given the nebulous purpose of this group, the dynamics within it, and a desire to assess the group's degree of success, measurable goals will be sought by members and the choice of these goals will be determined by whatever reliable measurements of behavior are possible. It is simple, for example, to count the number of new members and the variety among these in race, religion, age, appearance, education, personality, or values. Counts can also be made of the proportion of persons who talk during a meeting of that body, the kinds of persons who talk most or least, and the nature of accepting or rejecting actions shown most often and least often during face-to-face interaction among members (Bales and Cohen, 1979). Data may also be obtained by asking members to complete questionnaires or to be interviewed about their actions and attitudes in accord with the aims of that body. The respondents may be asked to rate how accepted they feel in the group or how constrained they are when approaching colleagues. Observations can also be made of the number of persons who leave the organization each year and how well new recruits resemble regular members. All such evidence, because it is measurable, soon inspires clear goals for members in these special matters.

Conceivably, persons who guide this group may use measures such as these when making an audit of the group's progress toward its goal. Whichever ones they use, some results are "better" than others because they are more in accord with the initial purposes of the group. If some outcomes are indeed better, what ones should members aspire to achieve? Selectors of the group's goals will recognize that forces to maximize the amount of interaction among all kinds of members are countered by restraints on that interaction and that these restraints originate in such matters as embarrassment, time available, energy, dislike for topics strangers wish to discuss, prior commitments, or outright incompatibility of one personality with another. In general, then, members will set the group's goal on each dimension as close to the ideal level as they think is reasonable in light of the forces that counteract efforts to attain that ideal. In practice, this probably means that members aspire for their group to be a bit more satisfying at each measurement period than it was previously. Such a criterion will seem sensible to members if they recognize that their cautiousness in mutual interaction decreases as their skill improves in approaching strangers and as they learn to know one another. Thus they can aim to improve the quality of their performance on each dimension. In summary, members choose from among all alternatives the most attractive goals that are reasonably possible for persons in their group to achieve because they are measurable and accessible.

Take, as another illustration, a group whose prime purpose is to change specific beliefs or behaviors of persons in the community outside the group. These power seekers may be employees in a department store pushing management to agree that salespersons should have a say in selecting what they sell, a college student council requesting faculty members in the department of history to change its curriculum, or a set of parents urging tobacco firms to tone down appeals to youth in their advertising. Members of a pressure group can tell whether their attempts to cause changes have been successful by watching for shifts away from the conditions they disapprove and toward ones they favor. How much movement in the target person's behavior can they expect and how rapidly? Considering the group's desires, they might ask for complete conformity to their demands. But agents of change also recognize that barriers can interfere with their efforts to introduce new ways.

Those who are put under pressure to change may protest, for instance, because they are opposed to the new idea. They may believe the change requires too much knowledge, skill, work, or expense; will not be efficient; is demeaning; or transgresses their values. They resist because they dislike the procedure or style used by those who propose the change. They may hesitate because they cannot confidently foresee how things will go when the new methods are in place. Or they may be anxious and uncooperative because the power sought by would-be agents of change, when granted to them, will perhaps be used in a way that limits the freedom of the influenced individuals (Cartwright and Zander, 1968; Zander, 1982).

Decision makers in a group that is trying to get nonmembers to adopt new practices must estimate which barriers exist and how strong these barriers are, when attempting to judge how far and how fast they can modify the behavior of the target persons. First, they will aspire to make in these people only those changes that seem possible without arousing their resistance. Next, they will try to reduce any resistance or actions counter to their aims. They might overcome opposition among target persons by presenting arguments in support of the planned change, using methods of persuasion that do not rile listeners, preventing uneasiness about future events by providing evidence to bolster their predictions on such matters, and reducing anxiety in persons being pressured by promising to use power in legitimate ways. The more that barriers to change are reduced, the more change the influencer can expect to generate and aim for. Third, they will increase the strength of their influence attempt by appealing to desires of those who are to be changed.

Members may offer incentives to target persons (such as greater profit, less strain, more harmony, or less waste) when the proposed changes are implemented. Members may coerce the target persons by threatening to create a repulsive situation (such as a strike, slow-down, resignation, or an increase in costs) if the proposal is not accepted. Or members may depend on their expertise, attractiveness, or trustworthiness to be the basis of their influence (French and Raven, 1959; Zander, 1982). Which they use depends on what they think is most likely to work. And this judgment, in turn, will affect their choice of a goal for the group.

In summary, the calculation responsible members make before attempting to set a goal for the changing of others considers the pressures they themselves can exert toward reaching that state, the strength of the barriers that target persons may put up against it, the chances of weakening these barriers, and the possibilities of increasing the weight of their demands. Plans to set a goal for bringing about change are shaped by the decisions of planners, on the one hand, and by the reactions of those who are to be influenced, on the other.

We might, in a similar manner, examine other desires of members for their group and how these can become bases for measurable and accessible goals. Additional desires might be members' interest in creating a group to foster colleagues' learning, healing, worshipping, emoting, mediating, punishing, obeying, prospering, or loving; feelings of security, awe, or excitement; or proper behavior. Motives of individuals, whether these are to satisfy self, to aid in the satisfaction obtained by others, or to generate satisfaction in the group as a whole, can determine the purpose of a group. There is much to learn, however, about how such a transformation from motive to purpose develops.

Summary

A motive is a capacity to find satisfaction in the attainment of a given incentive and a disposition to seek that satisfaction. A member may have a self-oriented motive or a group-oriented one (called a desire for the group). A group purpose or goal is an incentive. The strength of a motive is indicated by the tendency of a member to behave in accord with it. The strength of a tendency is determined by the capacity to be satisfied by a given state of affairs (motive), the existence of a state that, if attained, will provide more or less satisfaction (incentive), and an estimate of the chances that the satisfaction can be reached (perceived probability). The stronger the incentive, the perceived probability, and the motive, the more a person will act in accord with the motive. This is true regardless of whether the motive is for self alone or for the entire group.

The tendency of members to act for their group is determined by whichever is stronger—the desire to attain favorable outcomes for the group or the desire to avoid unfavorable ones. Members may wish that their group be successful, influential, nurturing, profitable, or a place for fun. When they have certain desires for their group, they choose for that body a purpose that will fulfill (or not violate) these intentions.

Ordinarily, if members are concerned with success by the group, they select a goal that will provide as much satisfaction as possible. This usually turns out to be one in the middle range of difficulty. If members are concerned with a motive other than group success, they become interested in having a measur-

able and accessible purpose so they can determine if and how
they may develop a satisfying state of affairs in those respects
for that unit.

Additional Readings

Carron, A. V. *Social Psychology of Sport.* Ithaca, N.Y.: Mouvement Publications, 1980. Contains an excellent review of
studies on the incentives people see for joining a sports team.

Locke, E. "Toward a Theory of Task Motivation and Incentives." *Organizational Behavior and Human Performance,*
1968, *3,* 157-189. A summary of studies on members' cognitive commitment to group goals.

Weick, K. *The Social Psychology of Organizing.* Reading, Mass.:
Addison-Wesley, 1979. Demonstrates that members in groups
often act first and find a purpose for their actions later.

Zander, A. *Motives and Goals in Groups.* Orlando, Fla.: Academic Press, 1971. Describes members' self-oriented and
group-oriented motives for achievement.

Zander, A. *Groups at Work: Unresolved Issues in the Study of
Organizations.* San Francisco: Jossey-Bass, 1977. Discusses
members' preference for more difficult goals and ways of
coping with embarrassment when a group does poorly.

EIGHT

Evaluating
and Changing
Group Purposes

In some units, participants hold fast to their group's purpose indefinitely. A study of thirty business managers in Yugoslavia and thirty in Peru, for example, showed that the purposes of their organizations remained the same over a period of seven years even though the workers' say in running the companies in Peru increased considerably, until it resembled the influence of workers in Yugoslavia (Hoover, Traub, Whitehead, and Flores, 1979). In contrasting groups, members select a new purpose for their unit whenever it becomes wise for them to do so. Why do some organizations stay with a fixed purpose and others modify their objectives?

Changes in Purpose

Consider instances of groups changing their aims. The committee for the senior prom finishes planning the dance and turns to running a campaign for one of their number who hopes to be elected president of the class. Ladies taking lessons in bridge cancel their instructions at midterm in order ro raise funds for the local playground. The staff of a mental hospital discharges patients from wards and moves them to homes in the community, giving these sick people their first anxiety-reducing medicines—a shift from monitoring deviant individuals to treating ill ones. A union buys a failing company and officers of that labor organization become managers who press workers for better productivity. A school of forestry broadens its interests and becomes a school of natural resources. The National Council of Churches transfers its emphasis from helping neglected individuals to assisting underdeveloped nations (Jenkins, 1977).

When participants recognize that changes in their group's goals may become necessary, they usually establish procedures to prepare for such moves. A political party plans to revise its platform before an election and holds workshops where members can suggest what these revisions might be. A city commission names new priorities based on suggestions of its long-range planning committee. The board of a fund-raising body sets a new goal for the amount of money it will collect after it has received requests from agencies that depend on that fund.

A group's acquired activities may be so unexpectedly rewarding that its original purposes are no longer given much attention. The Baldwin piano manufacturing firm, as an illustration, allows customers to buy its instruments on "time" and is so successful in this financial activity that the company becomes a lending and investing corporation in which the making of pianos is a less important matter. A volleyball team enjoys its conditioning program more than the game and becomes more devoted to body building than to competing. All in all, if members obtain satisfaction from working toward their group's purposes they stay with these. If not, they try to change them. Why this is so warrants study.

Events in the environment of a group can make its purposes ripe for revision. Some bodies, for example, make use of scientific information in their activities; and when technological developments occur, members recognize that their purpose is no longer useful—that different ends will be more suitable or that new ways of satisfying established aims are available. As a case in point, manufacturers of calculators used electronic chips when these came on the market and thus became producers of computers. Libraries no longer are merely lenders of books. They are now media centers for distribution of phonograph records, television tapes, moving pictures, microfilms of newspapers, computer programs, or slides of famous paintings. Citizens living in the neighborhood of a hospital ask for help in improving their health through advice about diet and exercise. Users of computers convince the telephone company to develop ways of moving their data over wire from one computer to another miles away.

Origins of Change

Although its purpose is the heart of a group's life, an objective can lose its hold. Perhaps conditions that originally stimulated its founding become less important to participants, and therefore the initial aim has less usefulness to them. A small college that was established in a city to educate the sons of Irish immigrants, as an example, gave up that purpose as the Irish were assimilated into being responsible citizens of the area. The school's faculty decided to find a new mission and eventually chose to concentrate on training business managers. The satisfaction that colleagues sought in a group when it was first organized may be fully met, and the group's initial purpose therefore has no remaining appeal for them. Working toward a group's purpose may have been gratifying to members at an earlier time but no longer is, and members lose their enthusiasm. Or they may see that the chances of success in reaching for the original purpose are poor, and they lose interest in that objective. Political parties often do this. Activities in a group may result in outcomes repulsive to individuals so that continued effort toward the group's goal does not seem wise: the probability of repeated losses is too great. Financial backers of a new play often must accept that their show will not appear on Broadway and will never return their investment.

When an organization has a given purpose, work toward that end can generate additional desires for the group. To illustrate, an association of cherry farmers in several counties pooled funds to start a research station where studies were to be done on growing better fruit. The results of their efforts also created interest in marketing, distributing, tree trimming, and harvesting. Association members now believe these new topics should be research interests too. A group's objective, in contrast, may be changed because efforts to reach its ends create side effects that cannot be tolerated. A commune aroused hostility among its neighbors because of its objectives. The members therefore changed their aims to make them more acceptable to critics.

The chief reasons, we believe, that a group's purpose comes to have little appeal to members and thus is vulnerable to revision (or neglect) are that it is ambiguous, has different meanings for different members, and provides no useful criterion when measuring whether the group is meeting its purpose. However, an obscure objective is not always removed from a group's by-laws simply because it is incomprehensible. Indeed, purposes in many going organizations are difficult to understand, attain, or measure. But when members keep a vague purpose, we have noticed, they eventually become inclined to ignore it in favor of a clearer other one. They prefer this more precise aim because their group exists to provide a particular kind of satisfaction for members and the participants cannot be satisfied unless they have an attainable goal, know what they must do to achieve it, and are aware of their accomplishment if and when they attain it. In short, an unmeasurable or inaccessible purpose yields little satisfaction; a clear one provides a favorable response even though it is a substitute for a vague purpose.

Putting it differently, members favor a measurable and accessible goal over an unmeasurable or inaccessible one because they seek satisfaction (or some degree of it) from fulfilling a goal and cannot attain that satisfaction unless they know how to do so. If a group's purposes are vague and members therefore do not see which paths to follow toward that end, they lose interest in these aims. If members cannot replace these objectives, they may no longer wish to retain membership in that body because it provides them little positive reaction. If the group's original purpose never was important to members and their desire for satisfaction from fulfilling it never was great, they probably will not bother to define a more measurable and accessible goal but will leave the initial one to be useless and ignored. If the prime purpose no longer interests members, they must find a desirable substitute for it, or the group will dissolve. It cannot survive without a viable purpose. It is well known that assembly-line workers who are given no group goals by management commonly create their own targets simply to reduce their boredom.

A change in a group's purpose represents an innovation for members. There are certain conditions under which such a new direction is most likely to be accepted within an organization. Rothman, Erlich, and Teresa (1976) accordingly reviewed writings on circumstances that determine whether people will agree to innovations. They offer the following generalization as a product of this review: "Innovations that are amenable for trial on a partial basis will have a higher adoption rate than innovations that necessitate total adoption without an anticipatory trial" (p. 23). They give evidence to support the idea that members are most accepting of change if they are given an opportunity to try out movement toward partial aspects of a new goal. On the basis of work by Rogers (1962), Rothman and colleagues propose that an innovation is most likely to be adopted if members have an opportunity to see the innovation in place and to witness what results it generates (*observability*) or if they employ a portion of an innovation before having to employ the total innovation (*trialability*). Furthermore, an innovation is most likely to spread if it is first used by a set of opinion leaders in that community.

Due to these ideas and their efforts to use them, Rothman and co-workers also propose the following guideline: "Practitioners wishing to promote an innovation in a general target system should develop it initially in a partial segment of the target system" (p. 25). Either a part of the innovation may be given a trial or the whole change may be tested on a section of the group. An incremental process is used; success on a small scale is taken as the basis for promoting the idea or for having it spread on its own among members. Apparently, the more a new goal can be visibly demonstrated, the more it will receive a favorable reaction from those with a stake in the goal.

Rothman and his associates suggest as well that "an organization's dominant goals reflect the influences of the most powerful individuals or groups in the organization and their vested interests" (p. 60). Based on this assumption, they offer a guideline for introducing changes in a group's goals: "Practitioners wishing to change an organization's goals may approach this problem through altering the structure of influence within the organization by either (a) increasing the power of those groups within the organization that hold goals compatible with the practitioners' or (b) introducing new groups into the organization that hold goals compatible with the practitioners' " (p. 61). Examples of (a) are the use of outside consultants, persuasion, or training of managers. Examples of (b) are unions, planning councils, or new sets of members.

Choosing a New Goal in a Working Group. When members are selecting a new level of quantitative goal because their unit has either reached or fallen short of its established target, they keep in mind that they have less chance of achieving a harder goal than of meeting an easier one. Even so, as we have noted, a more difficult end-state has greater appeal because members realize that they will develop more satisfaction in their group from achieving a higher aspiration and will feel prouder of their group if they attain such a level. They realize, too, that they will not be embarrassed for their group if it falls short of an objective more difficult than any the group has yet reached, but they will be embarrassed if they fail to reach an easy score. Therefore, the ultimate consequences are almost always better when striving toward a difficult goal: members develop more group pride if they succeed and less embarrassment if they fail. The opposite is true if they select an easy goal. Thus they usually aim for a more difficult goal rather than an easier one.

As a result of such considerations, members favor and select a goal that will provide as much satisfaction (after a success) or as little dissatisfaction (after a failure) as is possible for their group. The goal must be hard enough to provide satisfaction when achieved but not so hard that it can never be met. It should be, in sum, a moderate challenge—a goal that is not much harder than the best the group has so far attained. If the group succeeds on its objective, members next select a more difficult goal for the immediate future; if the unit fails, they do not change the goal's level but leave it at the place they were recently unable to reach. Over a time, therefore, a group's goals tend to be above the best previous scores of the group and these goals are conducive to further failure. Consequently, as already remarked, most groups fail to reach their goals more often than they accomplish them. They aim too high (Zander, 1971). One wonders how widespread this practice is in policy boards, planning commissions, legislative committees, and other course-setting entities.

When a group's purpose is based on a nebulous desire for the unit (such as power, nurturance, fun, harmony, or thoughtfulness), members do not assume that some goals are harder or easier than others. Rather, as we have seen, they try to define objectives that are as measurable and accessible as possible. Of these goals, they choose those that promise more satisfaction and less dissatisfaction from efforts to attain them. Goals that best fit approved values and most gratify relevant motives are likely to be most satisfying. Eventually, members' experiences in working toward a measurable goal make it possible for them to talk about group events in terms of preferred group states, both current and future. In turn, this allows them to appraise the chances of accomplishing that kind of objective and the attractiveness of doing so—just as they would on any task chosen from ones arrayed along a scale of difficulty. Better performance leads to better goals.

Pressures to Accept Particular Levels of Aspiration. Stimuli from outside a group induce members to change its goal if these external forces have a stronger impact on members' behavior than the group's established objectives. The influence of environmental conditions is stronger, we suspect, on groups that serve people outside it or that benefit from actions of outsiders than on groups that exist only for members' personal gains. Additionally, a demand on a unit will be more compelling when it is made by persons who legitimately have the right to influence persons in that body (Cartwright and Zander, 1968).

Imagine a working staff whose officers must reconsider

its goals regularly. The group might be an assembly line, a fund-raising organization, or a sales department. Studies of such teams in both natural settings and the laboratory show that members pay close attention to and are strongly influenced by inductions on their group directed toward a particular level of a group goal. These external pressures more often influence the group's new goals than do the unit's past scores. Four types of influence have been observed closely (Zander, 1971, 1977).

1. *Outsiders who depend on a group's product try to influence its goals.* Customers or suppliers, for example, request a company's officers to set a particular goal, or heads of departments seek to influence how much money will be allotted to their body by the firm's budget-setting committee and typically want more than they received in the past.

2. *Participants compare their group with ones nearby.* Members observe units with goals like their own; these might be similar companies, assembly lines, academic departments, or teams. When they learn the "score" of these units, they draw a parallel between their own record and the others'. As a result of such comparisons, participants wish to move their group's goals. They raise its objectives if they learn that other units have done better than theirs. But they do not lower their group's goals if other groups have done less well. A rival unit's successes have a greater impact on a group's goal-setting than do its failures. Comparison influences higher goals more than lower ones.

3. *Onlookers comment about a group's performance.* The commentators may be members of a relevant profession, writers of editorials, spokespersons for a consumers' association, or members of a legislative body. In a study of the effects that observers' comments had on a unit they observed, outsiders' predictions about the group's future had a stronger impact when they expected the group to earn a higher score than when they expected it to get a lower one. More precisely, goal-setting members raised their aims for the group when outsiders estimated the group would do well but did not lower their objectives when commentators said the group would do poorly.

4. *An individual who has the right to do so gives a direct*

order. A familiar example is a superior who asks a group of workers to reach a given level of attainment. More often than not, the superior wants an improved score from a group. In a slipper factory, managers set daily goals for each of two dozen assembly lines. These goals were not achieved 80 percent of the time, yet after a line failed, managers lowered the goal for the group only 20 percent of the time. The managers believed that difficult goals were a stimulus to hard work and that workers could reach them if they tried hard to do so. Surprisingly, when workers were asked privately what each thought the group's goal ought to be, the majority set their group's aspirations above the unreasonable levels requested by management (Zander and Armstrong, 1972).

Helping Members Choose Realistic New Goals. A goal that decision makers set for their group may be difficult or easy. Its difficulty determines whether a unit succeeds or fails in work toward that end, which in turn influences members' pride in the group. Ideally, a person will prefer a moderately challenging goal (neither too hard nor too easy) for the organization, one placed at a level just a bit higher than any the group has yet achieved. The following actions increase the probability that a challenging goal will be chosen by members (Zander, 1977).

1. *Obtain accurate measures of the group's performances and provide this information for decision makers in the unit.* For an activity that is repeated regularly (campaigns, contests, assembly lines), report the group's score after each trial. For an activity that is one continuous process (planning a building, constructing a bridge), report the group's movement as it finishes each major phase toward completion of its task. Such feedback of a group's accomplishments is necessary if members are to have rational expectations about its chances of future success. Without reliable evidence about the group's progress, members tend to think that their group is doing well even when it is not and tend to prefer goals typically chosen by successful groups (Zander, 1971).

2. *State the group's potential purposes, the reasons for its existence, as precisely as possible.* Direct activities in the

group toward fulfilling the organization's purposes. Provide each group activity with a clear goal if possible. Such a goal is used as a criterion for evaluating the group's performance in that function.

3. *Demonstrate to members that its goal is useful because it stimulates the development of good qualities for their organization.* Members perform better if they have a measurable aim than if they have an unmeasurable one. Treat the goal as an inducing agent that guides the direction of members' efforts and justifies collaboration among members. Use the goal to determine the distribution of rewards among members, whether all share alike in a common gain or whether some members get more than others.

4. *Encourage members to value the consequences of group success.* Do this by pointing to the attractiveness of conditions that follow a good performance and by emphasizing their importance. The exact nature of such consequences differs from group to group, but generally they promote members' pride in their unit and approval of their group.

5. *Increase the strength of members' desires for group success because persons who have more of such a desire develop a stronger preference for a reasonably challenging goal.* The desire is stronger among those who are greatly interested in attaining the satisfaction that follows a group success and who believe the chances are good that their group will succeed in its task. Thus members need a goal they want to reach and think they can attain.

6. *Play down any fear of what might happen if the group fails, and reduce members' concern about being embarrassed over the group's performance.* Reduce the wish to avoid group failure by increasing their desire for group success, stressing the significance of pride in the group, and improving the group's procedures and tools and the members' skills.

7. *Encourage members to compare their group's score with scores obtained by units similar to their own.* Take seriously any indication that their group's quality of output is poorer than that obtained by a rival.

8. *Try to have outsiders place reasonable but challenging*

demands on the group. Unreasonable demands can be advocated by an external person who is inclined to prefer very hard goals. Or the issuer of demands may in turn be pressed (by still others) to put difficult requirements on the group.

9. *Encourage members to introduce changes in the group that enable members to work effectively for their organization.* These changes improve the members' skills, the equipment available to them, or the group's management.

The purposes of a group may be modified because the priorities among these objectives are reordered. If a group's purposes are contradictory, for instance, conflict among them may be avoided by emphasizing first one and then another. As probabilities of achieving separate ends vary, or as their attractiveness rises and falls, participants in a group put some objectives ahead, leaving uninteresting ones aside. Douglas and Wildavsky (1982, p. 93) remark, "In hierarchies goals are multiple and vague, their multiplicity making it easier to satisfy different elements of the firm and retrospectively to rationalize whichever ones happen to be accomplished. Their vagueness facilitates agreement on changing direction without appearing to go back on commitments. . . . It is also unnecessary to meet all goals at once as if the firm were trying to solve a simultaneous equation. There is . . . sequential attention to goals, first one, then another. Moves are incremental, working with knowledge of levels achieved in the past to do a little more or less."

Members are more likely to change the purposes of their group when these have particular properties. It may be more possible, as a case in point, to change a measurable goal than an unmeasurable one or an accessible goal than an inaccessible one because it should be easier to see how one could manipulate and modify a clearer objective. Less important goals are also more readily modified because their low value provokes little resistance against changing them. Goals with weak power are revised more easily than ones with great power. Flexible objectives are, by definition, simpler to modify than inflexible ones, and targets that do not fit with others are more readily changed than those that supplement one another neatly. Objectives with less relevance to members' values or motives are easier to shift, we presume, because such aims have less anchorage in views that resist change. Goals with less acceptance among members are more vulnerable to change as well. Finally, as we have seen, very difficult or very easy ends are shifted more readily than those that offer only a modest challenge.

Preservation of Purpose

There are organizations, in contrast to those we have been examining, whose members make a point of holding to the same purposes indefinitely. Examples are officials of a religious body, trustees of an agency that serves personal needs of clients, a board of commissioners for a public utility, a committee with an assignment that takes a long time to complete, and administrators of a college. It is not uncommon for a group to underscore the value of such stability and to establish methods that protect against attempts to change objectives. An army follows established doctrine, a church conducts ceremonies that ask participants to revere its beliefs, a secret society pledges faith to its charter, and the coaching staff of a football team lays plans that fit its special system. A firmness of purpose is often guarded by officials who train members not to doubt the aims of the organization and who may punish persons who deviate from the set's objectives. Religious bodies and political parties are particularly likely to police the behavior of members in this way.

Some individuals feel most comfortable with things as they are. Churchgoers want interpretation of the gospel in terms that are familiar to them, citizens press city officials to keep their aims as these have been in the past, and customers complain if a store changes its inventory. Government agencies may disappear, but interested parties will try to make sure that their purposes are preserved. The initial objectives are passed on to a body whose life is continuing. According to Kauffman (1976), the disembodied purposes are thus transplanted and kept vital because citizens who benefit from the government's activities toward those ends press their elected representatives to maintain support for the objectives. Governmental agencies are not immortal, but their purposes appear to be. Perhaps there are also situations in which a group's purpose may best be served by dissolving the unit that originated them.

Change of any kind in a group, whether it be in its purposes, personnel, procedures, or projects, creates uncertainty about the future for members and for those who do not belong. This uneasiness is a source of resistance to change within an organization even when that shift is accepted as possibly beneficial to all. The sources of this resistance and how to overcome it are worthy of more research.

A group may persist in its prime purposes even when a change of course may be wise. Pressures from individuals in the group's environment can be directed against change and toward maintaining its objectives as they are. These resisters may be customers, workers, priests, bankers, or superordinates. The values of persons outside a group may remain fixed, thereby acting as barriers against revision in the group's plan. The motives of members for themselves or their group may stay as they were, providing no new stimulation for modifying objectives. Members may not put value in creativeness or innovativeness because they believe it is good to adhere to the fundamentals built into their organization. Resistance to change, in short, can outweigh interest in new purposes.

The purposes of a group may not be reconsidered if conditions that caused the unit's founders originally to create the body are already being served through efforts of that unit. Members of a union, for example, see that their solidarity has improved jobs in a workplace. A management committee knows from financial reports that it is running a successful firm. Those in a department for reducing air pollution are proud that they now can see the sky.

Some objectives in organizations remain unchanged because there is no way to tell whether their group is moving toward those ends. Do weekday services ensure saintliness among members of a congregation? Is the progress of a research organization furthered if its funds are equally divided among scholars? Does a company help the community by sponsoring a basketball team? Can a restaurant attract a better class of customers if it displays original paintings for sale on its walls?

Questions like these are hard to answer, and members can only guess whether these goals are being satisfied. Participants most often estimate, we suspect, that the group's objective is being satisfactorily fulfilled and ought not be changed because looking for success is more attractive than anticipating failure (Zander, 1971).

Sometimes the goal of a group is so clear that members can readily tell whether their unit has attained it, or the means for reaching that goal are so well delineated that members can see exactly what they must do to reach it. When this kind of specificity exists and a group performs poorly, their objective will not be changed because members will prefer to modify their group's methods rather than its mission in order to improve the chances of attaining the unit's aim.

Members will not bother to modify their group's purpose if they see it as a trivial or unimportant one and if the work required to change it will be more than is justified by the small gain to be made; old purposes based on long-forgotten values are examples of this. Or activities and programs for the body may be chosen on grounds other than requirements of that purpose, even though the purpose remains a part of the group's charter. A unit's objective that is not respected by persons outside it may invoke efforts among members to change the minds of its critics rather than the objective itself. In their book, *When Prophecy Fails,* Festinger, Riecken, and Schachter (1956) describe a religious sect that was organized initially to save its members, via a helicopter, from floods that would engulf the city of Chicago on a predicted date. Members developed renewed and even stronger attachment to this purpose after they had spent the designated night out in the cold waiting for the water and airborne transportation that never came. Once their prediction was shown to be incontrovertibly wrong, members decided to demonstrate that they were not incorrect after all by convincing doubters to accept the views of the faithful.

The properties of an organization's purpose determine whether members commit themselves to these objectives. We have proposed already that a group's goals are less likely to be changed if they are unmeasurable, inaccessible, unimportant, or trivial. We expect, as well, that objectives will less often be replaced if they strongly influence beliefs and behaviors of members or are themselves heavily affected by members' values or motives. Objectives in harmony and linkage with one another should be harder to revise than separate and contrasting purposes because each of the latter can be changed without affecting others. Purposes that concern outcomes for the group as a whole should be less changeable than goals that affect the separate fates of individual members.

Summary

The purpose or goal in some groups is changed whenever that seems wise. Any of a number of conditions cause members to lose enthusiasm for the group's initial interest and to seek a change: the circumstance that led to the group's formation is no longer important, members have their needs satisfied and thus need not support its aims, they find no more gratification from being a member, they believe the group is failing and will continue to do so, or the problem originally attacked by the group has been solved. Work toward an established purpose may create broader interests that members welcome for the group.

When a purpose is too vague, members prefer to work toward a more precise aim because they cannot find satisfaction unless they know how to attain the group's goal and whether they have in fact done so.

If the group's goal is to attain a certain level of achievement among a number of tasks arrayed along a scale of excellence, members raise the goal when they succeed and lower it when they fail. They commonly are influenced by external agents while choosing aims for their unit. They select a new objective that will provide as much satisfaction from a success and as little dissatisfaction from a failure as is possible. Goals tend to be higher than the group's level of performance, and therefore groups fail more often than they succeed. Responsible members can take a number of steps to ensure that a new objective is challenging to members—not too hard or too easy. Generally, these moves concern ways of obtaining useful information about the group's prior performance. If the group's purpose concerns matters other than achievement, members turn to goals that promise greater satisfaction and less dissatisfaction and prefer ones that are both measurable and accessible so they can assess their chances of fulfilling that group purpose.

Many groups hold to their purposes indefinitely whether or not they establish more measurable and accessible aims. The purposes and goals may not be changed if persons in the group's environment oppose a shift, members are against the change, the actions of the group are successful, the ends are too nebulous to evaluate or even modify, or the objective is too trivial to warrant the work required for a revision.

Additional Readings

Christopher, W. *The Achieving Enterprise*. New York: American Management Association, 1974. Describes how officers of a firm may discover appropriate new goals.

Cohen, M. D., and March, J. *Leadership and Ambiguity*. New York: McGraw-Hill, 1974. How the chancellor of a university can choose a fresh course for the total organization.

Jenkins, J. C. "Radical Transformation of Organizational Goals." *Administrative Science Quarterly*, 1977, 22, 568–586. A description of how and why a worldwide religious organization changed the direction of its efforts.

Rothman, J. L., Erlich, J. L., and Teresa, J. G. *Promoting Innovation and Change in Organizations and Communities*. New York: Wiley, 1976. An interpretive review of the common experiences people meet when trying to introduce changes in an organization.

NINE

Selecting
Group Programs
and Activities

Men in the Model Train Club conduct contests in which competing companies carry cargo from station to station on a schedule. Barbers at The Hairquarters trim the tresses of all comers. People at the Bay Marina sell, repair, and store boats. Ladies in the Women's Christian Temperance Union learn the effects of alcohol and teach their neighbors what they know. Persons on the planning committee in the furniture factory propose products their company might make in the future. Each assembly line at the slipper plant makes a different style of ladies' leisure footwear. And patients in a group for personal counseling try to understand, not judge, one another.

A group's programs and procedures are called its *activities*. These are conceived as paths to the group's goal because they help members move through physical or psychological space to reach a designated objective. An activity is created when participants plan what they will do, how they will carry it out, who will do what, the steps they must take against barriers along the way, and the resources they need to attain its completion. If these phases are properly followed, the group proceeds toward its goal.

After a bit of experience within an organization, if its procedures are not as efficient as they might be, members recognize that they should change what they are doing. As a result, they take steps in planning for the future. Ideally, these steps are made in a circular-causal sequence:

1. Decision makers establish an objective for the group and methods to be used in achieving it.
2. Action is taken toward that end, and these moves affect the group or conditions outside it.
3. Information about the output of the group is obtained and reported to deciders; this is called *feedback*.
4. These decision makers observe any deviation between the aim and the group's level of performance.
5. Desires members have for the group, their personal motives, and pressures arising from external agents affect members' reactions to this discrepancy.
6. If the deviation between outcome and expectation is greater than is tolerable, managers take steps to reduce the discrepancy by changing the nature of the activity, changing the group's objective, or both.

The important point is that the meaning of a group's performance is not simply something in the group's output itself or in the group as a whole; it is in the relationship between the performance and what is desired. When members obtain evidence about the group's accomplishment on each of a series of attempts, we can expect motivated behavior to be invoked as members seek to have their group improve (Zander, 1971).

Allan Wicker (forthcoming) has described the kinds of matters that must be cared for if a group (or any other situation that influences the behavior of individuals) is to come into existence. He believes that five types of resources must be made operable in such a case. A *resource,* as he sees it, is a state, person, or object that can contribute to a planned situation and is appreciated by those in that setting. The first resource is people, especially ones who know what is expected of them in that situation. Next are necessary tools, supplies, or equipment. Third is space appropriate to accommodate activities carried out there. Fourth is specific or general knowledge that bears on the group's operation. And finally come reserves of money, supplies, plans, or persons ready for use as needed. In order for a group to be developed, says Wicker, the required resources must be located, assembled at one site and time, and given a place in the program of the unit. This finding, organizing, and gathering of resources demands that organizers of a group devote time, energy, and money toward fulfilling the plan they have in mind for the group they intend to create.

Members probably change group activities more easily than purposes because activities are better defined, more comprehensible, and therefore easier to modify. Yet purposes probably determine activities more than activities determine purposes. Individuals resist changes in a group's activities if they have a stake in its programs, fear they will not be skilled in new efforts, and think they may lose status, respect, or rewards if a change occurs. Members may, moreover, dislike an ambiguous future more than they like a clear-cut present. Such uncertainty can be reduced if participants meet with persons who are planning to revise the group's activities, discuss the reasons for these revisions, consider how the new mode will be brought about, and prepare to cope with the effects of these changes. The discussants may also plan how to bring about new procedures in a way that is comfortable for both managers and members (Coch and French, 1948; Lippitt, Watson, and Westley, 1958; Cartwright and Zander, 1968; Rogers, 1962; and Rothman, Erlich, and Teresa, 1976).

Evaluating Activities

The defining of a group's aim becomes easier as members have more experience in working together and in evaluating their activities. These evaluations provide insight into what members reasonably can expect of a group's future performance and demonstrate to what extent group objectives were attained, its *effectiveness,* and at what cost, its *efficiency.*

Deniston, Rosenstock, and Getting (1968a, 1968b) describe methods of evaluating the work done by a staff of professional persons in a department of public health. The authors' notions illustrate how members of any work group can appraise their unit's progress. We borrow from the ideas of these writers in what follows. In their view, as in ours, a group activity is an organized effort to eliminate a problem, engage in a program, or attain a particular end. An activity requires three features: (a) specification of one or more objectives, (b) selection and performance of one or more actions toward those ends, and (c) acquisition and use of resources. Evaluating the effectiveness or efficiency of an activity requires systematic description and measurement of these three variables. A precise description of an activity in light of these terms is a statement that it consists of resources p, q, and r, used to perform actions x, y, and z that, in turn, are designed to attain objectives m and n. It is clear that different efforts can properly be called activities.

Given that one proposes to use particular resources in certain actions toward specified ends, the issue is whether achievement of an objective can be attributed to things done under the program. This is an evaluation of the *effectiveness* of that activity.

Analysis of activity effectiveness is simplified by using a set of ratios that involve the three variables, (a), (b), and (c), just noted. Some examples of these ratios are:

$$\text{Effectiveness} = \frac{(a) \text{ attainment of objectives due to action}}{\substack{(a) \text{ attainment of desired objective minus} \\ \text{status that would have existed in the} \\ \text{absence of the planned action}}}$$

$$\text{Effectiveness} = \frac{(b) \text{ actions actually performed}}{\substack{(b) \text{ actions that were to be performed,} \\ \text{according to the plan}}}$$

$$\text{Effectiveness} = \frac{(c) \text{ resources actually used}}{\substack{(c) \text{ resources that were to be used, according} \\ \text{to the plan}}}$$

The first ratio considers how well the group's objectives were fulfilled through activities intended for that purpose, setting aside goal achievements that might have occurred regardless of those intended actions. A United Fund may reach its financial goal in a campaign, for instance, because it receives a large unasked-for gift, not because its campaign solicitors sought and found enough funds. The attainment of the goal in this case is not a measure of how well the solicitors performed. The second ratio observes how much that had been planned for that group was actually carried out. A set of members who are busy but do none of the proper activities is not effective, according to this ratio. Such a measurement is especially important where programs are standardized, as in delivery schedules, care of hospital patients, or assembly lines. The third ratio examines the use of resources toward attaining the group's purpose compared with the plan or budget prepared for the use of these. A body that reaches its goal at more expense than expected is not effective. Many government agencies are said to do this.

Evaluations of activities in most organizations reveal that they seldom have complete success in attaining their objectives. Evaluations also show where problems exist in attaining full effectiveness. Our three ratios may be computed separately for each objective. If several objectives are in a time series and each is evaluated as just described, then the evaluator attains an indication of steps that need improvement in order to reach a given end. An activity may be less effective than initially intended for several reasons:

1. Assumptions linking objectives, actions, and resources are invalid.
2. Actions are not performed as planned.
3. Resources are not used as planned.
4. The goal is not measurable.

The *efficiency* of events in an activity must be of concern in any organization because there is a limit to the resources that can be assigned to each. In a group, *efficiency* may be defined as the ratio between the net attainment of objectives (an output) and the resources expended (an input):

$$\text{Efficiency} = \frac{(a) \text{ net attainment of objectives}}{(c) \text{ resources expended}}$$

The inverse of this ratio yields a measure of average cost:

$$\text{Average cost} = \frac{(c) \text{ resources expended}}{(a) \text{ net attainment of objectives}}$$

Efficiency studies can answer several other questions:

- What is the relationship between the attainment of objectives and the number and kind of actions conducted?

$$\text{Efficiency} = \frac{(b) \text{ actual actions performed}}{(c) \text{ actual resources expended}}$$

- What is the relationship between the number and kind of actions conducted and the resources expended?

$$\text{Efficiency} = \frac{(a) \text{ net attainment of objectives}}{(b) \text{ actual actions performed}}$$

Each of these ratios may be computed for portions of an activity related to each objective.

In a setting where the preceding measures are obtainable, administrators seek an acceptably high level of attainment at a minimum cost. From the relationships among these concepts, it can be seen that the degree of efficiency in an activity can be clearly interpreted only if the group's effectiveness is well understood. The efficiency of a sales staff can be better judged when we know how much it has sold.

Appropriate Versus Inappropriate Activities

Members who plan what their group is to accomplish and how it will do so perform better than those who act without any preplanning, say Weick (1979), and Miles and Randolph (1980). Members using an action-before-any-planning approach

learn more, however, than those who plan before they act because the former persons find it necessary, after a few trials on
the group's task, to figure out why things went well or poorly
for their organization. Miles and Randolph state that members
of a group become ready to replace its activities with new ones
if the unit earns an unfavorable evaluation of its performance,
influential members press for a change, there is time for members to reflect on needed modifications in their unit's activities, or participants have the resources to make revisions.

Appropriate activities in a group are those that lead
toward the group's objectives. *Inappropriate* activities lead elsewhere. Compared with its opposite, an appropriate activity requires members to complete fewer and simpler steps in order to
reach a satisfactory response; thus it is more *direct*. It calls for
less energy or fewer resources and therefore is less *costly*. It
can be completed more quickly and thus requires *less time to
complete* it. In sum, an appropriate activity tends to be a more
efficient means for fulfilling a group's objectives.

The efficiency or appropriateness of an activity can be
increased, suggests William Christopher (1974), if members decide what is to be done and how, under whose direction, and
by what deadline it is to be carried out. Christopher stresses the
importance of strategic thinking when planning an organization's activities. Such thinking develops while planners try to
answer the question, How do we get to our objective? *Strategy*
is the art of using available resources in order to achieve established objectives. These resources include people, time, physical
space, equipment, materials, energy, working capital, and information. Christopher holds that deployment of resources is a
fundamental commitment in planning for a group's future because once they are distributed they cannot easily be redeployed.
Among members, an appropriate activity generates more interest in attaining the group's goal because it promises a greater
probability of fulfilling that aim than does an inappropriate
one. Thus participants show more confidence in their moves,
and as they approach the objective, they become more certain
of the satisfaction they seek. An appropriate activity will probably generate a greater goal gradient, which is manifested by

members' greater enthusiasm and effort as they more closely approach the goal. Players on the winning team play better and better as the end of the game comes closer and closer.

An appropriate activity enables members to move better toward fulfillment of the group's purpose. The full effectiveness of a group may depend however on matters beyond mere achievement of the group's objective. Hackman (1985) suggests, for instance, that three criteria be used in assessing the effectiveness of a group: (1) the output of the group equals or exceeds a standard held by people who review its performance (their expectations are met), (2) the social process in the group helps members work together (the group is preserved as a cooperative unit), and (3) members' experiences in the group satisfy their personal needs (members are personally pleased by events there). Whether a group meets these three criteria depends, as Hackman sees it, on the effort members expend in working on their group's task, the amount of knowledge or skill members have for the task, and the appropriateness of the procedures members employ. Studies of organizations in Sweden by Bengt Stymne (1970) indicate that the quality of a group's processes is a major aspect of a unit's quality of performance.

The properties of an *inappropriate* activity ask members to move through more steps and more complicated ones than does an appropriate one. Thus the inappropriate activity is a more *indirect* path to the group's objective. It demands more effort of members and more resources; therefore it is a more *costly* course. It requires *more time* to reach the end point and is characterized as well by a poor fit, redundancy, or conflict with other activities in the group. In short, an inappropriate activity causes inefficiency.

When there is a choice between appropriate and inappropriate paths in a group, we expect managers to favor appropriate activities over inappropriate ones. Nevertheless, choice makers may select activities that, in the light of the group's objective, are not appropriate for that unit. To examine the origins of these choices, we take up a two-sided question: What conditions cause members to participate in appropriate activities and in contrasting ones?

Why Groups Have Appropriate Activities

Appropriate programs are most likely to be operating in a group if its purpose is measurable because persons who can measure whether the group has fulfilled its purpose can better determine which paths lead to that end. Likewise, they can more reliably select an appropriate activity if the purpose is accessible—that is, if they know the path to the goal at the outset. If the unit's purpose is important to individuals who have a stake in the group, managers of the body will want to move it toward that objective. They recognize that appropriate activities allow this better than inappropriate activities do. Members will prefer appropriate activities if they use problem-solving procedures because these methods give greater weight to reason than to emotion and because following a preordained path requires more contribution from the head than from the heart.

Officers of an effective group create sound problem-solving procedures so that the choice of its activities is wise. Typically, good problem solving moves through several phases.

1. *The problem that requires a response from members is described, and the reasons that a response is necessary are given.* This means that members decide what the group is to do in the light of the purpose set for it. In an effective group, one who presents the issue emphasizes its importance by describing adverse events that will follow if a solution for the question is not found. The presenter explains the significance of the issue, explains the kinds of information needed from members, and makes it clear what form of decision will be most useful. The initiator also suggests procedures to be used in working toward a decision. Conferees set up special procedures or pass the matter along to an expert or subgroup if the issue requires knowledge or treatment not at hand for them.

2. *A number of potential solutions are identified.* In this phase, members list and compare possible activities. The effectiveness of the group's effort depends on the soundness of the ideas developed.

3. *The best plan among available alternatives is chosen.* The quality of each proposed activity is tested by examining

whether the approach is in accord with the group's purpose and what side effects it may have if it becomes a chosen course. When confirming whether it is appropriate, members consider issues such as: What gains or losses will the group obtain from this activity? What gains or losses will persons outside the group obtain? How much will members approve or disapprove of their group after this solution? What will be the reaction of nonmembers? (Janis and Mann, 1977). The progress of a problem-solving process may be retarded because separate sets of participants will not give up contrasting notions. The one in charge of the discussion can prevent such polarization by pressing members to use each other's suggestions during the discussion so they are able to see where others' ideas lead and can give fair consideration to these.

4. *Action is taken to implement the decision.* Once a choice is made, members must give reality to the selected activities. These steps occur after the decision and are often assigned to persons who did not participate in choosing them. Thus implementers of the decision cannot fully know what was planned and why. These persons will resist taking action if they are not sure what they are supposed to do, if the proposed action does not resemble what they usually would do under such circumstances, if they do not see the importance of the steps they are asked to take, or if they lack the necessary resources, ability, energy, or time to do such things. Because movement toward the group's purpose may be slowed or blocked when implementers do not act, managers devote attention to ways of winning acceptance for the plans from persons who are to act on them. To that end, supervisors may invite implementers to attend the decision-making meetings, to decide how a decision made by others might be enacted, or both.

Plans to move a group toward its goal need implementation that goes beyond words of encouragement if members are to be stimulated. According to Hackman (1985), the group (in its personnel, standards, and procedures) must be properly designed for the job at hand. Hackman also expects members to work harder if their task requires a high level of skill, it is a meaningful whole, the results are visible to participants, the products are important to others, members have some say about how to do their work, and they receive reliable feedback about their group's output. Members also will work hard if rewards are given for the work of the unit as a whole, not for the production of separate individuals, and if members learn to coordinate their efforts while generating a shared commitment to the team and its work.

Members need to prepare what Hackman calls *appropriate strategies*. That is, they should lay out plans concerning who is to do what, and when. These procedures must be closely followed by workers, but the methods ought to be evaluated and changed when that is necessary. In order to appraise their procedures, members need reliable information at regular intervals about the quality and quantity of performance by their unit.

Why Groups Develop Inappropriate Activities

Clearly, the selecting of appropriate activities may be derailed if good problem-solving practices are not used while making the selection. Problems that members of a group encounter while planning group activities are discussed by Van de Ven (1980). These include recruiting of inappropriate staff, resistance to the group's efforts by persons outside the group, lack of sufficient resources, lack of clear plans, lack of knowledge about how to implement plans, and resistance among those responsible for putting these ideas into action.

Members support inappropriate programs for several reasons. One is that people who make decisions for the group are not able to judge the appropriateness of an activity because the group's purposes are not precise enough to guide that appraisal. If a group's objective provides little guidance, members' ideas about the group's activities will probably not fit together well because each person wants a group activity that satisfies his own personal interests. Members may settle these disagreements by bargaining, and the final choice is then often weighted with activities that meet members' private purposes; the group's needs are set aside.

An emphasis by participants on what they want to do as

individuals in order to improve themselves is likely to lead to inappropriate activities, but not if the group is a reflexive one that was created to serve the separate needs of individual members rather than the needs of the group as a whole. A group's procedures are usually laid out (when the group is reflexive) in such a way that each member can meet personal desires without conflict among participants. Thus activities in such a group tend to lean toward group discussion, cooperative doings, emotional support of one another, or other methods that limit strain among members and encourage interpersonal help. Self-therapy and counseling groups are examples of such bodies.

One cause for ineffective group decisions is called *groupthink* (Janis, 1972). This is a style of deliberating that members slip into when their desire to maintain friendly interpersonal relations overrides their good sense. Instead of choosing the most rational or appropriate plan (in the light of the group's purpose), they select one that best preserves harmony among them. In most cases, this decision is compatible with the way the group has done things and thought in the past. Not surprisingly, groupthink occurs most often in units with greater cohesiveness, where members are attracted to remain as members. Groupthink has five characteristics:

1. Members discuss only a few potential solutions and ignore other alternatives.
2. They fail to examine consequences that will follow their preferred course of action.
3. They too quickly drop suggestions that appear, at first, to be unsatisfactory.
4. They make little effort to get the advice of experts in the matter under discussion.
5. They fail to work out contingency plans to be used in case efforts to implement preferred ideas are waylaid.

Janis proposes a number of ways to prevent groupthink or to weaken its origins. In general, these methods are intended to ensure that discussants face facts, openly communicate with one another about these, and carefully consider adverse consequences of a potential decision.

Some persons talk more than others in a group meeting and thereby influence its decisions more even though their ideas may not be the best ones offered during the conference (Zander, 1982). An imbalance in the spread of participation is bad if the subject under discussion is one on which many members ought to have a say but do not feel free to do so. They may feel restrained because they do not understand the issue, are not interested in it, are afraid of making an observation that will be rejected by hearers, are intimidated by the size of the audience, or are awed by being in the presence of powerful persons. Activities in a group are typically undertaken by many members, and when an activity is being planned, it is wise if these people are given an opportunity to contribute their ideas and describe their experiences. If an unbalanced meeting limits verbal participation, the group's activities may become inappropriate.

When members of a group must deal with an emergency, such as a riot, storm, strike, or fire, they are prone to make errors in choosing a course of action either because the pressure of time makes them consider fewer options or because decisions are made by persons who are not expert in handling such a crisis. Moreover, during a critical period, information coming to the group is often of poor quality because messages sent in haste are either badly expressed or inadequately thought through. Under the anxiety created by stress, decision makers' behavior tends to be less flexible and imaginative than it might otherwise be (Holsti, 1971). For reasons like these, when members must hurry, a group's efforts are likely to be inefficient and not salient to its prime objectives.

A familiar cause for clumsy activities in a group is an attack on it by outside critics who have a vested interest in the results of its efforts. A city council, for example, considers whether to rezone an area of the city and is exposed to pressures by citizens who prefer a particular plan. A faculty committee debates whether research using hazardous materials should be allowed on the campus, and persons who oppose this research complain to the community that the committee is not giving the issue fair consideration—is giving extra weight to one side. Such criticisms can determine the group's decision. The eventual outcome may then be inappropriate because it reduces this external social pressure instead of resolving the original problem.

Some groups develop inappropriate programs because they need reliable information to make wise choices and these facts are not available. As a result, members are uncertain about what they can take for granted and how to evaluate their plans in choosing activities for the group. Their choice tends to veer away from the purposes of that body. A further source of inappropriate activities arises, we have seen, if the unit is repeatedly unable to reach its goal and members then wish to overcome their embarrassment. The goal is hard to achieve, not because it is ill-defined, but because it is at a level of difficulty that participants cannot attain. The group's failure causes members to place more weight on reducing their embarrassment than on improving their procedures or skill because there is a better chance of lowering embarrassment than of attaining success (given the unit's past record). They can reduce their embarrassment, we noted earlier, by continuing to choose an impossibly difficult goal for each repeat of the group's task (so that work toward the goal will be praised and failure to reach it will not be ridiculed). They also can declare that attainment of a goal is not worth the effort required, perceive external demands laid on the group to be simpler than they really are, deny they are embarrassed by the group's poor record, blame tools or methods used in doing the group's work, misrecall the group's scores so these appear better than those the group actually earned, or deny that members were at fault in their poor output. Thus steps taken primarily to reduce embarrassment are inappropriate; they do little toward ensuring a further success by the organization. A focus on lowering embarrassment for members will probably generate embarrassment for them again (Zander, 1977).

A final reason for inappropriate activities is that members become defensive, angry, or suspicious about demands or actions made of the group by persons outside the body. These reactions are not in accord with its initial purposes. Members who are convinced that their group's aims are right and noble often punish anyone who limits attainment of their objectives. Thus groups with a strong faith in the morality of their beliefs may act in immoral ways to defeat persons who disagree with them (Douglas and Wildavsky, 1982).

Summary

A group's activities are appropriate when they efficiently lead toward attainment of the group's objectives. These activities provide more direct, less costly, and briefer means for achieving the group's goals than inappropriate ones do. Appropriate activities help the group survive as a cooperative unit or satisfy personal desires for members. Appropriate activities are more likely to be chosen by members when the group's goal is more measurable, the goal is more accessible, specific activities have a higher probability of attaining the goal for the group, members prefer to be rational rather than emotional in their decisions for the group, and leaders of the unit help members employ sensible problem-solving procedures in making a choice of activity.

Inappropriate activities are more often established in a group when the group's purpose is not precisely enough stated to aid in making a decision about the group's activities, members prefer activities that will satisfy their personal interests rather than those of the group, negotiation among members to arrive at a common goal does not succeed, members prefer their separate personal objectives, discussants engage in a problem-solving process called groupthink, the views of a powerful subgroup dominate the choosing of activities for the group, urgency leads to errors in thinking among members, values are given more weight than facts in matters where an objective choice is needed, members take steps to overcome embarrassment in their group due to its poor performance in the past, and decision makers become defensive when discussing what their choice might be.

Additional Readings

Deniston, O. L., Rosenstock, I., and Getting, V. A. "Evaluation and Program Effectiveness." *Public Health Reports,* 1968a, *83,* 323–335. Offers a review of the variables involved in assessing the effectiveness of an organization.

Hackman, J. R. "A Normative Model of Work Team Effectiveness." In J. Lorsch (ed.), *Handbook of Organizational Behavior.* Englewood Cliffs, N.J.: Prentice-Hall, 1985. Identifies criteria one may use in evaluating the effectiveness of an organization.

Peters, T. J., and Waterman, R. H. *In Search of Excellence.* New York: Harper & Row, 1982. Describes what successful companies do to be successful.

Van de Ven, A. H. "Early Planning, Implementation, and Performance of Organizations." In J. R. Kimberly, R. H. Miles, and Associates, *The Organizational Life Cycle: Issues in the Creation, Transformation, and Decline of Organizations.* San Francisco: Jossey-Bass, 1980. Describes ways of selecting the procedures a group may use to attain its purpose.

Weick, K. *The Social Psychology of Organizing.* Reading, Mass.: Addison-Wesley, 1979. Proposes that a group's means are often more important than its ends.

TEN

Practical Lessons
for Group Leaders,
Consultants, and Scholars

We have reviewed a number of concepts a scholar might use in explaining the nature of a group's purpose. These ideas can also be employed in practical settings by persons who organize groups or help them to prosper. In this chapter, we recall relevant notions from prior pages and remark how these can guide researchers and developers of units as they try to understand or assist purposeful group behavior.

This chapter is addressed to three audiences. First, to organizers of groups, responsible members, or planners, all of whom we will call *organizers*. Second, to consultants, trainers, or specialists in the development of formal organizations, designated here as *facilitators*. And third, to students, researchers, or social scientists, identified as *scholars*. We direct our remarks to each of these types in turn. Our comments touch on several broad topics: the origins of groups, the selection of a group's purpose, and the use of group activities aimed toward this objective.

The Organizer of Groups

Not many years ago, a man in this county decided that our area needed a university for mature students who had to hold a job to support themselves and therefore could not attend classes full time. He went to the local bank and borrowed $2,000 to cover expenses he might meet in testing his idea. Soon he had a planning committee, which led to the appointment of a key staff, all of whom were housed temporarily in an abandoned mortuary. Today the school is an accredited institution with all the buildings and students it can handle. Organizations are similarly started every day. Generally, they are conceived to serve a useful function for the organizers, members, dependent outsiders, or society at large.

A person who thinks about founding a unit takes preliminary steps and gets others to help in these. At the outset, this person identifies what state of affairs is to be improved in members or surroundings, or what opportunity is to be seized. The condition the group is to modify must be well defined so that members are not asked to take part in group activities without knowing why they do so. Before creating a new unit, a developer has some idea about what conditions (to be created by activities of those in the group) will be more satisfying than the current ones and estimates the probability of attaining that state of affairs. Prior to proceeding, this individual must be convinced and assure colleagues that the proposed objective is reasonably attainable through their joint efforts.

The organizer who has the necessary authority may create a group unaided and tell designated members to accomplish certain goals in specified ways. Matters are more complex, however, when a developer recruits volunteers for a body that is being instigated with their help. To attract members to such a unit the organizer may put a story in the paper about the proposed group, giving the time and place for interested persons to appear; speak to likely candidates one by one and face to face; call a meeting and urge attendees to form a group; point out the likemindedness among persons and encourage their further association; circulate a petition calling for a new group; help a subgroup break away from a larger body; or tell a set of persons that they are to form a unit and then strengthen their perception of groupness by giving the assemblage attributes of a permanent body (Zander, 1982).

One who initiates a group prefers members who will help in establishing the kind of body being planned. The developer chooses, for instance, those persons who are more likely to participate in the body, understand the give and take required of a member, favor values that suit the group's activities and aims, forgo their own interests as needed for the good of the group, develop skills they must have for their role in the group, are attracted to individuals who already are members, and accept the group's purpose. Persons are trained in how to be members where this is necessary.

As soon as is feasible, moreover, an organizer finds answers to basic questions: What interests do members have, and which of these are most useful to the unit? How can colleagues be helped to cooperate with one another? Who will perform what duties for the ensemble? What procedures shall be followed in carrying out the group's programs? Who is to make the decisions? Who can be members? Who should be excluded?

If an organizer intends to create a large entity having hundreds of members, the early steps are not much different from those we have been reviewing because such an organization begins with only a few persons and slowly adds others. The planners for a bigger unit need to take care, however, in preparing certain matters, such as how work will be divided, authority will be shared, communications will move, new members will be socialized, procedures will differ in parts of the organization, and what criteria of effectiveness will be set up for sections of the whole.

An organizer does not always emphasize the purposes of a new group at the outset. This individual may meld persons into an informal unit without ever discussing with them the set's purpose in any detail or without naming a purpose that amounts to much. Such tentativeness in setting the body's objectives is most likely to happen if the activities of members directly reveal what the outcomes of the group will be, as in a sports team, a research unit, or a small shop. Many fairly purposeless units operate successfully simply because what members do becomes the group's prime reason for existing. But in the long run, members of groups that act before they plan for these actions come to want a better understanding about what they are doing and why they are doing it. In most organizations, the group's purpose is exactly defined before planning for the body begins, and this objective is a valuable attribute when a developer is trying to get persons to join the group or to deepen their involvement in it. The purpose of a group is discussed more extensively when persons are being recruited than at any other time. A developer usually assumes that joiners want their group to have a purpose because it helps members answer basic questions like: What standards of achievement are appropriate for this body? Can I fulfill my personal goals through membership? Are my services useful to this organization? Are my aims compatible with the targets of this group? How will my performance be evaluated? What programs are most suitable for this unit to sponsor?

A developer helps members become interested in a group's purpose by doing several things. Events are arranged in such a way that participants have to interact with and depend on each other in a group task, as in planning a special project, repairing a broken object, or completing a big joint job. Participants thereafter see themselves as a whole; each person's gain helps others as well. Or a developer may demonstrate to members how the success of their group is threatened if they are competing when they should be collaborating. An organizer takes it for granted that members dislike disagreeing about the purpose of their group and that they will be willing to work toward defining a common view of this objective. When members reach a decision on what the group's purpose is to be, the results of their conferring will be acceptable to them, and they will press one another in the future to abide by this agreement.

The method members use in choosing a purpose for their group can affect the quality of their choice. In order to stimulate the thinking of decision makers, a group's manager learns what comparable bodies are planning to do, reports this information to colleagues, sets a time limit for completing their decision, describes an unfeasible ideal that the group should approach as closely as possible, and does not worry about inconsistencies among separate selected objectives. The manager may propose particular purposes for an experimental trial period to see how well they work and ask deciders to have more faith in their intuition than they ordinarily would. The Delphi procedure, although unwieldy, provides a more detailed decision than one made in a face-to-face meeting. Advice on methods to use in selecting group objectives is found in writings by Christopher (1974), Cohen and March (1974), Janis and Mann (1977), Van de Ven (1980), and Zander (1982).

A purpose decision makers choose for their group ordinarily conforms to their values, even though choosers of a purpose are not always aware that values guide this decision. If they later discover that their group's purpose is contrary to their beliefs about right and wrong, they change the purpose, ignore it completely, or leave the group; the value is usually left as it is. Early in the formation of a group, a wise developer observes what values are most important to members and then the developer sponsors purposes and activities that fit these opinions. Over time, values change among members and others who have a stake in a group, and an organizer changes the group's purpose accordingly. The group will benefit if its manager recruits persons whose values are similar to ones members of the organization already honor.

Members bring to a group a capacity to be satisfied by certain outcomes and a disposition to seek such satisfaction; this is called a *motive*. A motive may be what a person wants as an individual, wants for the group as a whole, or both. Different motives arise in different people at different times. An organizer can teach a person to value a particular motive, arouse that motive, or suppress it—whatever may be most useful in getting a new group under way. A sponsor of a group tries to have members satisfied with that body or at least not dissatisfied with it. In order to do this attractive incentives are created for them as attributes of the group being organized. An *incentive* is a state or outcome that provides satisfaction when attained by a person. A group's purpose is an incentive for members when the objective is a task to be achieved by the group as a whole or when the unit tries to create a state within it, such as fun, sympathy, courage, reverence, or social support. The incentive of a group's purpose is less important to members when the group exists primarily to help participants fulfill their own private plans. In such a case, a manager mainly offers help, encouragement, and resources for members so they can do their own thing and need not be concerned about the effect of their acts on outcomes for the group as a unit.

One who develops a group increases the incentive value of its purpose by assuring members that they can fulfill that objective and will be satisfied when they do so. Members become more willing to work toward a group's objective, moreover, when they have a stronger desire for their group to succeed. An organizer can arouse this group-oriented motive among members by emphasizing for them the importance of having pride in their unit, the sources of this kind of satisfaction, and what consequences pride has for participants and the ensemble as a whole. The developer helps members feel favorable toward their group by getting responsible persons to set clear and challenging goals, making sure that members aid one another, and by facilitating a good performance in the ensemble. Persons responsible for choosing a group's purpose will select one that promises as much satisfaction and as little dissatisfaction as possible.

In all walks of life, some tasks are harder for a group than others in light of the experience and talent available to that collection of persons. Anyone who helps a group select work-relevant goals must keep in mind that members prefer more difficult objectives over easier ones because participants can be more satisfied if they achieve a difficult goal than if they reach an easy one and will be less embarrassed if they fail on a stiff task than if they miss on a soft one. Usually, a target that is a bit harder than their best success so far (but not too hard) induces the most effort from members.

When persons define a group's purpose they automatically give it certain properties that cause consequences for the group just as the substantive content of the purpose does. Take, for example, measurability of purpose. In a body that has work to accomplish, it is helpful if attainment of the group's goal is measurable so that members can understand what they must do to fulfill it. In a body devoted to creativity, fun, and friendship, however, there is less need for a measurable purpose. Indeed, a too precise goal may make members' activities so rigid that their creativity, fun, or friendship cannot flower. A vague purpose is more sensible than a clear one if members want to take part in varied activities and do not wish to be pinned down to a specific direction, want an objective that presents the group's image well, or need to cover up activities that ought to be kept out of sight. In a majority of instances, however, members and managers will not be comfortable with an obscure group purpose. They will prefer measurable and accessible goals that they can substitute for a nebulous one and can better use to guide their group's and their own activities.

As long as a group's purpose is viable, a manager helps members hold to that objective. This is done, as we have remarked, by assuring them of satisfaction if and when they attain that end. If it becomes desirable to prevent a change in the purpose of the unit, the manager creates or tries to benefit from conditions that keep a group's objectives resistant to change. Examples of these are opposition among interested nonmembers to modification in the group's purpose, protests by members against such a shift, success by the unit in fulfilling the current aim of the group, or constraints to keep the group's current objectives because they best suit the values of the community. Despite a leader's efforts, circumstances can cause members to lose interest in the unit's original objective: events that inspired the group's formation are no longer at issue, members have had all the satisfaction they need, the group is a failure in moving toward its goals, or new intentions arise out of experience in the group. When members' enthusiasm decreases, managers are responsible for diagnosing its cause and for deciding whether the group should hold its course or change its direction.

Given that the organizer of a group creates it for a particular function, that individual will foster activities there that are in accord with that objective and will try to measure the effectiveness and efficiency of these programs. To be sure that the group's program is appropriate for the unit's target, the developer must satisfactorily answer issues such as the following before members are enlisted to act in behalf of the body. What gains or losses will the group meet in this activity? What gains or losses will persons who are not members obtain? How much will participants approve or disapprove of their group after this effort? What will be the reaction of outsiders to these events? The organizer can confidently expect that members will like their deeds better when these are more appropriate to the aims of the group. Nevertheless, persons may feel that attainment of its established objective is not a true indicator of a unit's quality of performance. They also may wish to judge the goodness of their group on the basis of additional signs of goodness in the unit's activities, such as whether events within the group generate harmony among members, members can depend on one another, they are pleased by their experiences in the group, or they feel the group's procedures have few adverse side effects. When responsible persons have settled on a group's purpose and have begun activities toward that end, they need to make accurate assessments of the group's attainments periodically so they can initiate adjustments in the group's objectives and can base its programs on reliable feedback.

The Facilitator of Group Operations

The value of a facilitator is based on two characteristics: (1) expert knowledge about the operations of groups because of training and experience and (2) an ability to generate objectivity when seeking facts about the unit without revealing a vested interest in or an evaluation of these data. Decisions about a group's purpose, recruits, socialization of members, activities, or performance can be more reliable if a facilitator observes (and comments on) a discussion of these matters by responsible members.

Topics treated in this volume are often behind the problems that clients present to a facilitator. Complaints about ineffectiveness of the group, loss of interest among members, competition where there should be cooperation, pettiness of goals, decrease in morale, unreliable measurement of progress, weak programs, or violations of members' values are issues familiar to specialists who help organizations improve themselves. Depending on the exact nature of the problem presented, an advisor will find it useful to examine the group's purposes and members' motives. Consider some examples.

A common cause for difficulty in a group is that it lacks a sound purpose. Either there is no stated objective at all, or the description of it is so obscure that it is not a good guide for members. In such a case, an advisor aids a group by pressing responsible persons to recall what problems or opportunities initially led to formation of the body. Once this causative situation has been delineated, the facilitator helps them recall what state of affairs they wanted to attain through joint collaboration; that is, what objective they set for the group and why. The consultant assists participants, moreover, to understand the nature of measurable and accessible purposes and why these are valuable in work groups. The counselor may also guide group decision makers when they determine what properties of a newly chosen purpose will be most suitable for their organization. Two questions suggested by Christopher (1974) help members work toward a definition of their group's identity: What is this group? What should it become? A facilitator will find that the client organization wants to improve such matters as its ways of recruiting members, selecting activities for the group, bettering its procedures, creating a supportive work environment, teaching members the skills they need to be effective, showing supervisors how to manage by objectives, and giving members confidence that they can attain the ends they seek for the group and themselves.

A virtue of facilitators is that they can observe in a group things that members and managers are not able to see because of their close involvement in the work of their unit. If a group's purpose is disapproved by members because it violates their values, a consultant can help managers identify which values members prize the most and which ones are being transgressed. Such assistance is useful for a group because members become uncomfortable (often without knowing why) when they note that the purposes of their organization are not proper.

An outside consultant contributes to a group by making

an assessment of members' motives. Such a consultant may make a survey of members' interests among potential programs in that group, administer a test of their needs, review with them their satisfaction in that body, study their complaints, or analyze how matters might be improved. These several approaches amount to the same thing: The advisor is trying to determine members' wishes and how the organization can provide an incentive for these motives. A counselor may identify what state of affairs would lead to the best fit between the needs of members and the purpose of the group or may suggest ways of improving this fit. Such an individual can help groups be sure that their goals are not too hard or too easy and can assist them in making rational choices in these matters. This person can ferret out sources of members' resistance to change in the group's purposes, can spot activities that are appropriate or inappropriate for the group, and can determine why these are supported even when they are not sensible there. Finally, the counselor can, in the absence of sensible group purposes, advise members in procedures they may follow so that, after the fact, they may eventually identify objectives for useful actions (Weick, 1979).

Topics for Further Research

Ideas in this monograph may stimulate scholars to study aspects of purposive behavior in groups. In order to encourage such an interest I offer a list of topics that warrant investigation.

- Why are the purposes of groups often stated ambiguously? Do the division of labor among members of groups or contrasts in members' private interests interfere with exactitude in the thinking of persons who are describing the group's purpose?
- How do members react to a group's purpose when they have little interest in it? Are they likely to give meager help toward accomplishing that group objective? Or are they more likely to withdraw from it? Do they tend to give more weight to their personal desires than to the goals of the

group when the group's objective is not attractive to them? If a group's intention is to help members accomplish their personal aims, how do members react if they do not welcome such assistance?

- What is the conceptual nature of a characteristic of a group purpose? Are the properties described in Chapter Four appropriate ones? What additional properties are noteworthy?
- We assume that people prefer a group that has a measurable and accessible purpose. But this preference is not always strong because many groups, such as patriotic societies, poetry reading circles, religious congregations, or fraternal orders, have vague purposes, yet they successfully attract and hold members. How come?
- One reason that units with nebulous aims hold their members is that participants invent precise goals as surrogates for vaguely stated initial goals. They set up these substitute objectives because such targets are more understandable, members know how to work toward them, and participants can tell when they have attained them. Are vague goals disliked by members because participants cannot tell what they must do to obtain satisfaction for themselves or the group when they take part in the units' programs?
- The power of a group purpose in controlling the behavior of members depends in part on the perception among them that colleagues in the unit accept that purpose. In uniformity of view, it is assumed, there is strength (and credibility). The power of a purpose also depends on the strength of a member's desire to fulfill the purpose. Which of these two— agreement among many persons or their motivation to reach an objective—is the stronger? Under what kinds of conditions?
- In what circumstances is the potency of a group's purpose more influential for persons than the members' own personal desires? Their own accomplishments?
- Which values have the most weight in what kinds of groups? How do values influence the process of decision making and goal selecting in a group? Do a group's values operate in ways similar to the motives it most prizes?

- What is the precise relationship between an individual's self-oriented motives and that individual's desires for the group as a whole? Can a group's purpose serve as an incentive for a person? If so, what conditions make this most likely to occur? How shall we conceive of a member's secret plans that covertly influence that person's public behavior as a member?
- Under what circumstances is a member likely to lose interest in a group's purpose?
- What are the typical steps organizers follow when creating a group? What is the conceptual meaning of these steps?
- How often, and in what kinds of situations, are members most likely to act before they think about a goal for group-oriented actions?

References

Allport, G. W., Vernon, P. E., and Lindzey, G. *A Study of Values*. Boston: Houghton Mifflin, 1951.

Ansoff, H. I. *Corporate Strategy*. New York: McGraw-Hill, 1965.

Atkinson, J. W., and Feather, N. *A Theory of Achievement Motivation*. New York: Wiley, 1966.

Bales, R. F., and Cohen, S. P. *SYMLOG: A System for the Multiple-Level Observation of Groups*. New York: Free Press, 1979.

Barnard, C. I. *The Functions of the Executive*. Cambridge, Mass.: Harvard University Press, 1938.

Berscheid, E., and Walster, E. H. *Interpersonal Attraction*. Reading, Mass.: Addison-Wesley, 1978.

Boorstin, D. J. *The Discoverers*. New York: Random House, 1983.

Borman, L. D. "Help Yourself and Others Too." *The Rotarian*, 1983, *143*, 12-15.

Burns, T. "The Reference of Conduct in Small Groups: Cliques and Cabals in Occupational Milieux." *Human Relations*, 1955, *52*, 166-170.

Carron, A. V. *Social Psychology of Sport*. Ithaca, N.Y.: Mouvement Publications, 1980.

Cartwright, D., and Zander, A. *Group Dynamics Research and Theory*. New York: Harper & Row, 1968.

Caves, R. E., and Uekusa, M. *Industrial Organization in Japan.* Washington, D.C.: Brookings Institution, 1976.

Christopher, W. *The Achieving Enterprise.* New York: American Management Association, 1974.

Coch, L., and French, J. R. P. "Overcoming Resistance to Change." *Human Relations,* 1948, *11,* 512-532.

Cohen, M. D., and March, J. *Leadership and Ambiguity.* New York: McGraw-Hill, 1974.

Cook, D. L. *Program Evaluation and Review Technique.* Cooperative Research Monograph, no. 17. Washington, D.C.: Bureau of Research, United States Department of Health, Education and Welfare, 1966.

Cyert, R. M., and March, J. G. *A Behavioral Theory of the Firm.* Englewood Cliffs, N.J.: Prentice-Hall, 1963.

Delbeca, A. L., Van de Ven, A. H., and Gustafson, D. H. *Group Techniques for Program Planning.* New York: Scott, Foresman, 1975.

Deniston, O. L., Rosenstock, I., and Getting, V. A. "Evaluation of Program Effectiveness." *Public Health Reports,* 1968a, *83,* 323-335.

Deniston, O. L., Rosenstock, I., and Getting, V. A. "Evaluation of Program Effectiveness." *Public Health Reports,* 1968b, *83,* 603-910.

Deutsch, M. "The Effects of Cooperation and Competition Upon Group Process." *Human Relations,* 1949, *2,* 129-152, 199-231.

Douglas, M., and Wildavsky, A. *Risk and Culture.* Berkeley: University of California Press, 1982.

Drucker, P. F. *The Practice of Management.* New York: Harper & Row, 1954.

Durant, W. *Our Oriental Heritage.* New York: Simon & Schuster, 1935.

Durant, W. *The Life of Greece.* New York: Simon & Schuster, 1939.

Durant, W. *Caesar and Christ.* New York: Simon & Schuster, 1944.

Durant, W. *The Age of Faith.* New York: Simon & Schuster, 1950.

Durant, W., and Durant, A. *The Age of Louis XIV.* New York: Simon & Schuster, 1963.

England, G. W. *The Manager and His Values: An International Perspective for the United States, Japan, Korea, India, and Australia.* Cambridge, Mass.: Ballinger, 1976.

Etzioni, A. *A Comparative Analysis of Complex Organizations.* New York: Free Press, 1975.

Feather, N. *Expectation and Actions.* Hillsdale, N.J.: Erlbaum, 1982.

Festinger, L., Schachter, S., and Back, K. *Social Pressures in Informal Groups.* New York: Harper & Row, 1950.

Festinger, L., Riecken, H., and Schachter, S. *When Prophecy Fails.* Minneapolis: University of Minnesota Press, 1956.

French, J. R. P., and Raven, B. "The Bases of Social Power." In D. Cartwright (ed.), *Studies in Social Power.* Ann Arbor, Mich.: Institute for Social Research, 1959.

Funk, D. A. *Group Dynamic Law: Integrating Constitutive Contract Institutions.* New York: Philosophical Library, 1982.

George, C. S. *The History of Management Thought.* Englewood Cliffs, N.J.: Prentice-Hall, 1968.

Georgiou, P. "The Goal Paradigm and Notes Toward a Counter Paradigm." *Administrative Science Quarterly,* 1973, *18,* 291-310.

Gross, B. M. "What Are Your Organization's Objectives?" *Human Relations,* 1965, *18,* 195-216.

Hackman, J. R. "A Normative Model of Work Team Effectiveness." In J. Lorsch (ed.), *Handbook of Organizational Behavior.* Englewood Cliffs, N.J.: Prentice-Hall, 1985.

Holsti, E. R. "Crisis, Stress, and Decision-Making." *International Social Science Journal,* 1971, *23,* 53-67.

Hoover, J. D., Traub, R. M., Whitehead, G. J., and Flores, L. G. "Organizational Goals in the Peruvian Co-Determination and the Yugoslav Self-Determination Systems." In G. W. England, A. R. Negandhi, and B. Wilpert (eds.), *Organizational Functioning in a Cross-Cultural Perspective.* Kent, Ohio: Kent State University Press, 1979.

Janis, I. "Group Identification Under Conditions of External Danger." *British Journal of Medical Psychology,* 1963, *36,* 227-283.

Janis, I. *Victims of Groupthink.* Boston: Houghton Mifflin, 1972.

Janis, I., and Mann, L. *Decision Making*. New York: Free Press, 1977.

Jenkins, J. C. "Radical Transformation of Organizational Goals." *Administrative Science Quarterly*, 1977, *22*, 568-586.

Kanter, R. *Commitment and Community*. Cambridge, Mass.: Harvard University Press, 1972.

Katz, D., and Kahn, R. *The Social Psychology of Organizations*. New York: Wiley, 1966.

Kauffman, H. *Are Government Organizations Immortal?* Washington, D.C.: Brookings Institution, 1976.

Kets de Vries, M. F. R., and Miller, D. *The Neurotic Organization: Diagnosing and Changing Counterproductive Styles of Management*. San Francisco: Jossey-Bass, 1984.

Lanternari, V. *The Religions of the Oppressed*. New York: Knopf, 1963.

Lebra, T. S. *Japanese Patterns of Behavior*. Honolulu: University of Hawaii Press, 1976.

Lewin, R. "Santa Rosalia Was a Goat." *Science*, 1983a, *221*, 636-639.

Lewin, R. "Predators and Hurricanes Change Ecology." *Science*, 1983b, *221*, 737-740.

Lippitt, R., Watson, J., and Westley, B. *The Dynamics of Planned Change*. San Diego, Calif.: Harcourt Brace Jovanovich, 1958.

Locke, E. "Toward a Theory of Task Motivation and Incentives." *Organizational Behavior and Human Performance*, 1968, *3*, 157-189.

Mager, R. F. *Preparing Instructional Objectives*. Belmont, Calif.: Pitman Learning, 1962.

Mager, R. F. *Goal Analysis*. Belmont, Calif.: Pitman Learning, 1972.

Malcolm, S. M. "Within the Community of Scientists." *Science*, 1984, *224*, 48-49.

Maslow, A. *Motivation and Personality*. New York: Harper & Row, 1954.

Mayer, A. "The Significance of Quasi-Groups in the Study of Complex Societies." In M. Banton (ed.), *The Social Anthro-*

pology of Complex Societies. London: Tavistock Publications, 1966.

Miles, R. H., and Randolph, W. A. "Influence of Organizational Learning Styles on Early Development." In J. R. Kimberly, R. H. Miles, and Associates, *The Organizational Life Cycle: Issues in the Creation, Transformation, and Decline of Organizations.* San Francisco: Jossey-Bass, 1980.

Newcomb, T. *The Acquaintance Process.* New York: Holt, Rinehart & Winston, 1961.

Olson, M. *The Logic of Collective Action, Public Goods and the Theory of Groups.* Cambridge, Mass.: Harvard University Press, 1971.

The O. M. Collective. *The Organizer's Manual.* New York: Bantam, 1971.

Parsons, T. *Structure and Process in Modern Societies.* New York: Free Press, 1960.

Perrow, C. "The Analysis of Goals in Complex Organizations." *American Sociological Review,* 1961, *26*, 854–866.

Peters, T. J., and Waterman, R. H. *In Search of Excellence.* New York: Harper & Row, 1982.

Pfeiffer, J. *New Look at Education.* Poughkeepsie, N.Y.: Odyssey Press, 1968.

Raven, B., and Rietsema, J. "The Effects of Varied Clarity of Group Goals and Group Path upon the Individual and His Relation to His Group." *Human Relations,* 1957, *10*, 29–44.

Rogers, E. *The Diffusion of Innovations.* New York: Free Press, 1962.

Rokeach, M. *The Nature of Human Values.* New York: Free Press, 1973.

Rokeach, M. *Understanding Human Values: Individual and Societal.* New York: Free Press, 1979.

Ross, D. K. *A Public Citizen's Action Manual.* New York: Grossman, 1973.

Rothman, J. L., Erlich, J. L., and Teresa, J. G. *Promoting Innovation and Change in Organizations and Communities.* New York: Wiley, 1976.

Ruffner, F. G. (ed.). *Encyclopedia of Associations.* (5th ed.) Detroit, Mich.: Gale Research, 1968.

Scott, W. *Values and Organizations.* Skokie, Ill.: Rand McNally, 1965.

Scott, W. G., and Hart, D. K. *Organizational America.* Boston: Houghton Mifflin, 1979.

Scott, W. R. *Organizations: Rational, Natural, and Open Systems.* Englewood Cliffs, N.J.: Prentice-Hall, 1981.

Seashore, S. "Criteria of Organizational Effectiveness." *Michigan Business Review,* 1965, *17,* 26-30.

Seashore, S., and Yuchtman, E. "The Elements of Organizational Performance." Unpublished paper, Institute for Social Research, Ann Arbor, Mich., September 1966.

Shaw, M. *Group Dynamics, The Psychology of Social Groups.* New York: McGraw-Hill, 1981.

Stein, A. "Conflict and Cohesion: A Review of the Literature." *Journal of Conflict Resolution,* 1976, *20,* 143-172.

Stinchcombe, A. L. "Social Structure and Organizations." In J. March (ed.), *Handbook of Organizations.* Chicago: Rand McNally, 1965.

Stone, C. *Where the Law Ends.* New York: Harper & Row, 1975.

Stymne, B. *Values and Processes—A Systems Study of Effectiveness in Three Organizations.* Lund, Sweden: Studentlitteratur, 1970.

Swanson, G. E. *The Birth of the Gods.* Ann Arbor: University of Michigan Press, 1960.

Tajfel, H. "Experiments in Intergroup Discrimination." *Scientific American,* 1970, *223,* 96-102.

Thibaut, J., and Kelley, H. *The Social Psychology of Groups.* New York: Wiley, 1959.

Thomas, E. J., and Zander, A. "The Relationship of Goal Structure to Motivation Under Extreme Conditions." *Journal of Individual Psychology,* 1959, *15,* 121-127.

Toch, H. *Social Psychology of Social Movements.* Indianapolis, Ind.: Bobbs-Merrill, 1965.

Tocqueville, A. de. *Democracy in America.* Vol. 1. New York: New American Library, 1956. (Originally published 1835.)

Tocqueville, A. de. *Democracy in America.* Vol. 2. New York: New American Library, 1956. (Originally published 1840.)

Vaill, P. B. "The Purposing of High Performing Systems." *Organizational Dynamics,* 1982, *11,* 23–39.

Van de Ven, A. H. "Early Planning, Implementation, and Performance of Organizations." In J. R. Kimberly, R. H. Miles, and Associates, *The Organizational Life Cycle: Issues in the Creation, Transformation, and Decline of Organizations.* San Francisco: Jossey-Bass, 1980.

Wallroth, C. "An Analysis of Means-Ends Structure." *Acta Sociologica,* 1968, *11,* 110–118.

Warriner, C. K. "The Problem of Organizational Purposes." *Sociological Quarterly,* 1965, *6,* 139–146.

Weick, K. *The Social Psychology of Organizing.* Reading, Mass.: Addison-Wesley, 1979.

Whitely, W. "A Cross-National Test of England's Model of Managers' Value Systems and Their Relationship to Behavior." In G. W. England, A. R. Negandhi, and B. Wilpert (eds.), *Organizational Functioning in a Cross-Cultural Perspective.* Kent, Ohio: Kent State University Press, 1979.

Whyte, W. H. *The Organization Man.* New York: Simon & Schuster, 1956.

Whyte, W. K. *Small Groups and Political Rituals in China.* Berkeley: University of California Press, 1974.

Wicker, A. W. "Behavior Settings Reconsidered: Temporal Stages, Resources, Internal Dynamics, Context." In D. Stokols and I. Altman (eds.), *Handbook of Environmental Psychology.* New York: Wiley, forthcoming.

Wieland, G. F. "The Determinants of Clarity in Organizational Goals." *Human Relations,* 1969, *22,* 161–172.

Zander, A. *Motives and Goals in Groups.* Orlando, Fla.: Academic Press, 1971.

Zander, A. "The Purposes of National Associations." *Journal of Voluntary Action Research,* 1972, *1,* 20–29.

Zander, A. *Groups at Work: Unresolved Issues in the Study of Organizations.* San Francisco: Jossey-Bass, 1977.

Zander, A. "The Origins and Consequences of Group Goals." In L. L. Festinger (ed.), *Retrospections on Social Psychology.* New York: Oxford University Press, 1980.

Zander, A. *Making Groups Effective.* San Francisco: Jossey-Bass, 1982.

Zander, A. "The Value of Belonging to a Group in Japan." *Small Group Behavior,* 1983, *14,* 3-14.

Zander, A., and Armstrong, W. "Working for Group Pride in a Slipper Factory." *Journal of Applied Social Psychology,* 1972, *2,* 193-207.

Ziman, J. *Reliable Knowledge.* Cambridge, England: Cambridge University Press, 1978.

Index